SECURING THE NATION

ISSUES IN AMERICAN NATIONAL SECURITY SINCE 9/11

Intelligence: The Human Factor

Maritime and Port Security

Narcotics and Terrorism

MARITIME AND
PORT SECURITY

SECURING THE NATION

ISSUES IN AMERICAN NATIONAL SECURITY SINCE 9/11

MARITIME AND PORT SECURITY

Captain Fred Evans

Series Consulting Editor
Larry C. Johnson
CEO, BERG Associates, LLC
Washington, D.C.

CHELSEA HOUSE
P U B L I S H E R S
A Haights Cross Communications Company

Philadelphia

CHELSEA HOUSE PUBLISHERS
VP, New Product Development Sally Cheney
Director of Production Kim Shinners
Creative Manager Takeshi Takahashi
Manufacturing Manager Diann Grasse

Staff for MARITIME AND PORT SECURITY
Senior Editor Tara Koellhoffer
Production Editor Megan Emery
Assistant Photo Editor Noelle Nardone
Series and Cover Designer Keith Trego
Layout 21st Century Publishing and Communications, Inc.

A Haights Cross Communications Company

www.chelseahouse.com

First Printing

1 3 5 7 9 8 6 4 2

Library of Congress Cataloging-in-Publication Data applied for.

ISBN 0-7910-7614-8

CONTENTS

INTRODUCTION

The horrific attacks of September 11 changed forever our generation's sense of security. Although terrorism is not a new phenomenon, most Americans thought of terrorism as something that showed up in Hollywood movies. International terrorists rarely carried out attacks inside the United States. We were complacent.

When the first plane hit the northern tower of the World Trade Center, our complacency vanished. We now understand in some measure what our grandparents and great-grandparents felt when Pearl Harbor was attacked. We have felt firsthand the shock, bewilderment, confusion, and fear that they certainly felt upon hearing that the U.S. Navy's fleet at Pearl Harbor was bombed on Sunday morning, December 7, 1941.

Our own "date which will live in infamy," however, was more traumatic—not because more people died, but because we all witnessed the terrible events. Unlike our grandparents, most of whom learned of Pearl Harbor through secondhand sources—the radio or newspapers—we saw it happen live and, initially, unfiltered. We shared part of the experience of the people who were actually at or near the World Trade Center or the Pentagon on that fateful morning. Everyone who was near a television witnessed the burning buildings, the collapsing towers, and the fleeing crowds. We did not have to *imagine* fear, for we *saw* it.

The shock of the event was accompanied in short order by an overwhelming sense of vulnerability and the start of a search for how this could happen. Fear remained a dominant emotion. Images of troops in the streets in Washington, D.C., and New York City and combat air patrols by jet fighters reinforced the impression that we were under siege. Rather than venture out of the house, many stayed home. Airports and train stations were vacant. Business travel and tourism dropped precipitously.

In the succeeding months we have become acquainted with color-coded threat systems and witnessed the creation of new government institutions, such as the Transportation Security Agency and the Department of Homeland Security.

September 11 transformed America and its citizens. As the shock subsided and we coped with our fears, our attention shifted to explaining how the attack had been accomplished, punishing those responsible, and fixing the vulnerabilities that had enabled the attack to succeed. Americans—citizens and pundits alike—began asking questions: What would it take to make the United States truly secure? Is security a realistic objective, or are we chasing an illusion? What is the nature of the threat or threats that we are confronting? To stop religious extremists, are we willing to empower the federal government to spy on churches, mosques, or synagogues? How can we achieve effective national security and still remain a free people?

The books in SECURING THE NATION may not provide complete answers to these questions; some questions probably cannot be answered at all. But these books *will* equip the reader with knowledge about the security changes that are currently under way in the United States and will enable the reader to think and speak intelligently about issues of national security.

We are living in a historical moment, a period of time during which an event or series of events sets in motion forces that will shape the future, the world of the next generation. The bombing of Pearl Harbor, the Holocaust, the destruction of Hiroshima and Nagasaki by atomic bombs, the assassination of President John F. Kennedy in November of 1963—all were historical moments. The terrorist attack of September 11 and the invasion of Iraq both are historical moments. We are living in the midst of changes that years from now will be viewed by our children or grandchildren as watershed events.

COULD 9/11 HAVE BEEN PREVENTED?

Were the 9/11 hijackings an unexpected "bolt from the blue"? No, not really. Even though most Americans were unfamiliar with Osama bin Laden, Al Qaeda, and the radical Islamic terrorist training camps in Afghanistan, the intelligence community and the law enforcement community were well aware of these threats. Have you ever tried to put together a jigsaw puzzle? If you have the pieces of the puzzle, you can assemble the picture with concerted effort. If pieces are missing, the puzzle will be impossible to complete. In the aftermath of 9/11 we discovered that we'd had the clues all along, that information on the threat posed by bin Laden and his followers had been collected—but that those clues had been scattered among different government agencies and organizations. The agencies had not shared their puzzle pieces with one another.

A more specific example of this "failure to communicate" can be found in the Bojinka plot of 1995. In January of that year, Philippine police and firefighters accidentally stumbled upon a group of terrorists trying to make explosives in their apartment in downtown Manila. The subsequent investigation revealed that this group included one Abdul Basit, the man who had planned and carried out the first bombing of the World Trade Center in February of 1993. Basit managed to elude the Philippine police, but one of his partners, Hakim Murad, was arrested. When Murad was interrogated by Philippine police he revealed that he, Basit, and three others had planned to plant bombs on commercial jets and blow them up in mid-flight. The conspirators had intended to execute their plot, which they had code-named "Bojinka," toward the end of that same January.

This information was passed to the Federal Bureau of Investigation (FBI), which was assisting the investigation. The FBI considered as its mission to gather evidence that could ultimately be presented before a judge and jury in order to convict the terrorists—not to share this information with other agencies. Neither did the FBI feel that it had a responsibility to warn American air carriers about the possible attack. Many FBI agents involved with the case believed that sharing this information would compromise the FBI's case and prevent the prosecution of the terrorist in custody.

Meanwhile, Central Intelligence Agency (CIA) operatives in Manila discovered the Bojinka plot and published an intelligence report. The report was then disseminated throughout Washington agencies and departments, including the Department of State, the Department of Defense, and the Federal Aviation Administration (FAA). This CIA report sparked a dispute among the agencies over whether to inform the American air carriers about the threat; at a meeting convened in late January, representatives from the various departments argued heatedly over what to do with this information. The FBI feared that releasing the information to the airlines would compromise its ability to prosecute the terrorists who had hatched the plot and was therefore strongly against sharing. For the State Department and the FAA, the goal was to use intelligence to warn the airliners about a threat and to take steps to prevent the attack. Thus the FBI was pitted against the State Department, the FAA, and the CIA; ultimately the decision was made to warn the airlines. No attack is known to have occurred.

This story of the discovery of the Bojinka plot and the

uphill battle to share the information obtained from the investigation illustrates the processes and bureaucratic cultures that allowed 9/11 to happen. I am not assigning blame or fault to any particular organization. Rather, I want to emphasize that although we have one government, it is made up of a variety of departments and agencies, each of which has a unique way of looking at the world. It is possible for each department to work to the best of its ability to do its job properly but, in the end, only help to create a disaster. The law enforcement mentality sees its task as one of acquiring and preserving evidence with the ultimate goal of convicting a suspect in a court of law. The work of a criminal investigation is compartmented—in other words, only those directly involved with the case will have access to the evidence collected. Given that an organization like the FBI conducts thousands of criminal investigations every year, it becomes easy to appreciate that no one person or group of persons can fully understand the various cases being pursued.

In the aftermath of 9/11, we learned more disturbing facts. An FBI office in Minnesota had tried unsuccessfully in August of 2001 to obtain a subpoena to examine a computer used by Zaccarias Moussai, who was taking flying lessons but had shown no interest in learning to perform takeoffs or landings. Earlier in 2001, the FBI office in Arizona had submitted a request to investigate foreign Muslims who were taking flying lessons and acting suspiciously. This request also had been rejected. Then we learned that the FBI's debriefing of Hakim Murad in January 1995 had revealed that the terrorists had planned to hijack commercial airliners in the United States and fly them into CIA headquarters—and we came to the sickening realization that we'd had key clues in our hands and had not understood them or acted on them. Many law enforcement agents had recognized the potential threat, but their efforts to attract attention to the information had been blocked by bureaucratic procedures and also by individuals who had not appreciated the magnitude of the threat.

The intelligence community failed to process the clues and act in time to prevent the attack; here again, as with the example of the FBI, we have learned that there was plenty of information available. In January of 2001, for example, CIA officers in Malaysia monitored a meeting that included individuals who later hijacked the planes on 9/11. The CIA claims its agents passed this information to the FBI, but it appears that the intelligence was sent through an informal e-mail. In order to be taken seriously, information sent between agencies must be sent in the proper format. In this case, the informal nature of the communication resulted in the information's "falling between the cracks."

From the perspective of the intelligence community, it is important to protect information in order to hide the identity of the sources. Unlike the FBI, which is focused on collecting evidence to build a specific case, the intelligence community generates volumes of more general information. Genuine intelligence analysts are paid to sift through the information flood and to extract important data, much like a gold prospector who crouches over a stream for hours at a time, filtering out mud and water to find the occasional nugget of gold. But the task is greater than just *collecting* the information; the pieces of intelligence must also be assembled, analyzed, interpreted, and molded into a coherent story.

The ability of CIA and FBI analysts to predict or even fully analyze terrorist threats has been restricted, however, by limitations on the kinds of intelligence these agencies can collect and analyze. In the late 1960s and early 1970s, President Richard Nixon ordered the FBI and the CIA to gather information about his political enemies, and these abuses led to reforms that prevented the FBI from collecting intelligence on American citizens without evidence of a possible crime. The reforms also limited the CIA's ability to operate domestically; consequently, the powers of the CIA and FBI to conduct domestic intelligence activities were scaled back dramatically. Since then, the CIA has focused its attention and resources on threats outside the United States, and the FBI has emphasized building specific cases for prosecution. In the years before 9/11, no agency or department of the United States government had the power to collect and analyze intelligence about terrorist activities *within* the United States that were being directed by *foreign-based* entities.

The problem of information sharing between the FBI and the CIA becomes even more profound once we understand that the law enforcement community and the intelligence community both comprise multiple agencies. The law enforcement community, for example, includes the U.S. Customs Service, the Drug Enforcement Administration (DEA), the Internal Revenue Service (IRS), the Secret Service, the U.S. Marshals, the Bureau of Alcohol, Tobacco, Firearms, and Explosives (ATF), and the U.S. Park Police. Each agency has the power to conduct federal criminal investigations, and no central system exists to organize all the information the agencies collect. In fact, there have been numerous instances in which multiple agencies pursued the same target. In 1991, for instance, DEA agents arrested Dandeny Muñoz ("La Quika") Mosquera for drug trafficking and money laundering. Mosquera, who had planned the bombing of an Avianca commercial airplane in Colombia in November of 1989, also was the target of an terrorist investigation led by the FBI. Rather than cooperate in the investigation, the two federal agencies pursued the target independently, with DEA winning the race.

The intelligence community, though not as large, is equally diverse. In addition to the CIA, there is the Defense Intelligence Agency (DIA), the National Security Agency (NSA), the National Reconnaissance Office (NRO), various intelligence outfits in the

U.S. military's regional commands, the Department of Energy (DOE), and the FAA. The CIA, DIA, NSA, and NRO specialize in intelligence collection, which means they use either human spies or technology to intercept signals. Once this information is obtained, it is turned into a finished product, much like a newspaper article, and distributed to policymakers and intelligence analysts in other organizations. In highly sensitive cases, however, there is some information that is not shared with other organizations.

The law enforcement and intelligence communities both knew that Osama bin Laden and his followers were responsible for previous attacks and were planning future attacks. Unfortunately, the hunt for bin Laden and the effort to prevent future attacks were neither coordinated nor focused: Each organization pursued the target using its own resources and according to its own goals. In the mid-1990s, for instance, the government of the Republic of the Sudan offered to hand bin Laden over to American authorities. The offer was handled primarily by the Department of Justice and the Department of State, rather than through a "full-court" effort by the entire government. According to one of those involved in brokering the potential deal, it fell apart over the fact that no one at the Justice Department believed a solid, prosecutable case could be brought against bin Laden based on the evidence available at that time.

After 9/11, we learned that there were numerous serious indicators of an impending attack but that the information had been scattered among too many agencies to form a meaningful picture. Parts of the Al Qaeda network had even been penetrated by the U.S. government, but we had failed to pay attention to available intelligence and to act on it in a decisive, coordinated way.

Thus there were *two* important failures that paved the way for 9/11—not only the failure to share information between the intelligence community and the law enforcement community, but also a failure of analysis. We had the key pieces of the puzzle, but we failed to put them together. Because of these twin failures, the Twin Towers collapsed, the Pentagon was partially burned, and a plane fell in a Pennsylvania field after valiant passengers struggled to wrest control of the aircraft from its hijackers.

PUNISHING THOSE RESPONSIBLE

The terrorist attack of September 11 awakened the slumbering United States from years of apathy. We discovered in early 1995 that Osama bin Laden was linked to the terrorists who had bombed the World Trade Center in 1993. With attacks by Islamic militants against the U.S. military's housing complex in Dharan, Saudi Arabia, and the August 1998 bombings of the American embassies in Kenya and Tanzania, it became clear that we were at war with bin Laden. Bin Laden and his followers, who were based in Afghanistan, were training warriors for *jihad*—Islamic holy war against Western infidels—and plotting new offensives. President Bill Clinton launched cruise missile strikes against Al Qaeda training facilities in August of 1998, but the missile strikes inflicted little damage on the terrorists. When they attacked the U.S.S. *Cole* off the coast of Yemen in October of 2000, the United States did nothing. The terrorists considered the United States a weak nation, one incapable of defending itself.

It was not until nineteen Islamic militants simultaneously attacked the nation on September 11 that the United States found the motivation to mount a significant response. President Bush and his national-security team immediately began to plan the nation's strategy. The immediate problem was the terrorist training camps in Afghanistan, so within days U.S. intelligence and special-operations personnel were on the ground in that country. They forged ties with opponents of the

Taliban, the main regime that was harboring bin Laden and his
Al Qaeda followers. Two months after the September 11 attack,
U.S. military operations were under way in Afghanistan,
successfully routing both the Taliban and Al Qaeda.

The success of the war in Afghanistan proved to be the first
and least difficult phase in the "war on terror." Not only were
the training camps destroyed, but American forces captured
Islamic radicals, documents, and computers that in turn
provided law enforcement and intelligence with an information bonanza. Unlike previous failed efforts, the FBI and CIA
now joined forces to work together in genuine partnership. An
interagency team established operations centers throughout
the upper floors of the J. Edgar Hoover Building, the FBI's
headquarters, which sits six blocks east of the White House.
In addition to FBI agents, the task forces were staffed by
representatives from U.S. Customs, the Department of the
Treasury, the ATF, the IRS, the Secret Service, the U.S. Marshals,
the NSA, the CIA, the DOE, and the NRO. It was a veritable
"alphabet soup" of government agencies and an important
attempt at cooperation.

With the destruction of Al Qaeda training camps in
Afghanistan, the number of viable military targets for counterterrorist operations decreased dramatically. As a result, the
focus shifted to intelligence and law enforcement operations,
both domestic and international. The investigation of Al
Qaeda revealed a multilayered organization with support cells
and adherents in numerous countries. Working with foreign
police and intelligence operatives, U.S. agents set to work in
hundreds of regions around the world. Financial investigations
revealed covert support to terrorist operations from Islamic
charities based in the United States. Other terrorists were
caught engaging in more mundane criminal activities, such as
cigarette smuggling.

The capture of key members of Al Qaeda provided further

leads in the search for additional collaborators. A few of those apprehended were subjected to conventional arrest, and many more are being held in military detention centers. Since 9/11, the United States has entered new legal territory in several domains, among which is prisoners' rights. The terrorists in custody are treated humanely according to the standards of the Geneva Convention, but they are denied the legal rights granted to prisoners of war. By removing the terrorists from society, the United States has disrupted their ability to plan new attacks, recruit new followers, and kill more innocent civilians; it is no coincidence that in 2002 international terrorist attacks fell to their lowest level in 34 years.

FIXING THE VULNERABILITIES

The lack of information sharing between and among government agencies and the failure to act on information in our possession were not the only shortcomings that the 9/11 attack revealed. In the aftermath, we finally acknowledged that many of our security systems were inadequate and under-funded. For example, the hijackings were *not* a consequence of inadequate work by security screeners; in fact, the security companies that guarded the screening checkpoints at Logan and Dulles airports did their job properly and permitted on the aircraft only items that were acceptable by existing security standards. Before September 12, 2001, modeling knives were allowed aboard commercial airliners.

The Al Qaeda terrorists did not defeat the aviation security systems that were in place on September 11, so much as exploit the gaps in those systems. Although not heavily armed, the terrorists ensured that at least four members of their group were aboard each plane. They selected domestic flights with the full understanding that international flights would be more likely to be guarded by air marshals. They also knew that they did not *have* to be heavily armed. They could hijack a plane simply by announcing an intention to do so and threatening the pilots, flight attendants, and passengers—brandishing even something as innocuous as a fountain pen or a cylindrical tube.

The aviation security system of the time was based on the belief that even if someone hijacked a plane by threatening to detonate a bomb, the crew, especially the pilots, would stay in control of the plane because hijackers were not pilots. September 11 exposed this assumption as false. Not only had some of the hijackers undergone training as pilots, but they also were suicidal—preserving their own lives was *not* among their goals.

The flight crews on 9/11 acted in accordance with their training. They did their jobs bravely. Pilots and flight attendants had been taught to handle hijackers in much the way that a bank teller is taught to deal with a bank robber—to cooperate, to surrender what the aggressor wants, and to stall as much as possible in the hope that reinforcements will arrive. On 9/11, we learned the hard way that this training was not a valid way of handling a modern hijacking—and that fuel-filled planes could very easily be transformed into human-controlled cruise missiles.

Since the 9/11 hijackings, the federal government has been taking concrete steps to prevent such a thing from ever happening again. Aboard the commercial airliners, there was a fundamental shift in the ways in which flight crews were taught to respond to a hijacking. Rather than cooperating and granting hijackers access to the cockpit, pilots now remain behind a locked door. The doors have been hardened to withstand, albeit temporarily, attempts to open them, even those attempts that use bullets or hand grenades. A hardened door buys the pilots time; with luck, the extra time will enable them to take the aircraft down to an altitude that will minimize the risk of a catastrophic decompression if the skin of the aircraft is breached. In addition, pilots now are authorized to carry a pistol and have the last-resort option of being able to open a lockbox, remove a handgun, and defend the plane from being taken over if a hijacker succeeds in bypassing the door.

Significant changes in aviation security have also occurred on the ground. The responsibility for security screening has been taken away from private contractors and put into the hands of the U.S. government's new Transportation Security Agency. Money has been appropriated to purchase and deploy explosive-detection systems to check luggage for bombs. Passengers traveling by air today have a much greater guarantee that the trip will be safe and more secure.

Improving aviation security was relatively easy because a "roadmap" for the process already existed. Previous reports issued under both Republican and Democratic administrations—the *Report of the President's Commission on Aviation Security and Terrorism* (1990) and the *White House Commission Report on Aviation Safety and Security* (1997) had identified the problems and recommended solutions.

But securing the nation is not a simple proposition, and there is no easy "roadmap." America's sense of vulnerability was magnified by 9/11 and by the wave of anthrax attacks that followed it—which remain unexplained even now. Regardless of the cause, the spate of infections highlighted the fact that the existing system for handling and delivering postal mail did not include safeguards or systems for detecting and preventing the movement of hazardous materials. The federal government responded rapidly by installing equipment to detect and disinfect suspicious mail. Also, new measures were adopted for improving communications with local public-health departments and the Centers for Disease Control and Prevention (CDC), the main federal institution charged with protecting the public from disease.

Out of this chaos, the Bush administration conceived of a

broader vision of national security. In a move that recalls the National Security Act of 1948, which led to the creation of the Department of Defense and the Central Intelligence Agency, the Bush administration proposed establishing what it called the Department of Homeland Security. This federal department consists of agencies drawn from the Department of the Treasury (e.g., the Secret Service, the U.S. Customs Service), the Department of Justice (e.g., the Immigration and Naturalization Service), the Department of Transportation (e.g., the Coast Guard, the Federal Aviation Administration), and the Department of Energy. In theory, the new department will provide any administration with the ability to establish a clear security budget for protecting the nation. This reorganization is intended to reduce the overlap in agency activities and enable the federal government to focus scarce resources on specific problems.

With the arrival of the Department of Homeland Security comes a central mechanism for dealing with a variety of security tasks that previously were dealt with in a haphazard, uncoordinated way. The responsibility for ensuring that there are plans and standards for protecting nuclear power plants, seaports, public transportation (including buses, subways, and commuter trains), public water systems, and electrical grids is now fairly straightforward. This does not mean that the task is simple, though. The Department of Homeland Security represents a collection of agencies and personnel, and the difficulty of managing it will rival the challenge of managing the Department of Defense.

Less dramatic but equally important reforms are under way at the CIA and the FBI, the FBI's transformation being the greater of the two. Before 9/11, for example, documents and records that the FBI obtained in the course of a criminal investigation would lie dormant in boxes; they were never converted to electronic files that could be searched using current data mining technology. Under the leadership of Robert Mueller, the FBI has established a unit on the top floor of its headquarters, the J. Edgar Hoover Building, that is dedicated to scanning the millions of documents that the agency collects. The database resulting from this scanning effort is large already and growing. It offers to investigators a previously unavailable resource for finding links between terrorists and mundane criminals. In addition, the FBI has set up several different task force operation centers that are staffed around the clock and include representatives from other agencies.

President Bush also directed the FBI and the CIA to create a joint threat-monitoring and threat-assessment center. Both agencies initially resisted this plan, but both relented under persistent pressure from the president and his advisors. Providing one place where threat information from domestic and international sources can be evaluated cooperatively and analyzed for links will bridge the gap that enabled critical warning intelligence to go unnoticed in the weeks and months prior to 9/11.

CONCLUSION

The books in SECURING THE NATION provide a comprehensive introduction to the changes that have taken place in American national security since the terrorist attack of September 11. The current issues in national security are discussed by experts who have worked extensively to resolve those issues. Certainly, there is nothing wrong with an academic viewpoint—but theoreticians who have no grounding in practice often have difficulty in finding the roots of the issues they study. The authors in this series, in contrast, are thoughtful practitioners. They have served their country as military officers and government officials. They have grappled with the problems of developing and implementing new policies amid intense bureaucratic battles. Some have been sent on top-secret missions by presidents—many of which remain highly classified.

As you read and debate the information in these books, I encourage you to think critically. The publication of a piece of information does not make that information true. Be quick to ask why, and insist on hard, empirical evidence to corroborate or refute a statement claimed as fact. Hopefully, you will discover that national security is not based on deploying the most technologically sophisticated metal detector or hiring thousands of new specialists—but on freedom and the rule of law. The freedoms we enjoy belong to citizens who know their rights and understand how their government works.

The surprise attack on Pearl Harbor in 1941 produced a reaction of fear, a fear that ultimately was invoked to justify confiscating the property of Japanese Americans and jailing them in concentration camps. Even though the United States was at war with Germany and Italy as well as Japan, the federal government targeted only citizens of Japanese heritage, possibly because they were the most "different." The September 11 hijackers were Islamic radicals from Saudi Arabia and Egypt, so 9/11 created a similar opportunity to target Arab Americans. The Bush administration made a conscious effort after 9/11 to ensure that Arab Americans were not defined as a threat, so the nation was not subjected to another episode of internment or widespread persecution. But the analogy illustrates the need for citizens to understand issues of national security: Lapses in security can and *have* been used to justify restricting the civil liberties of American citizens. Consider the ideas in these books, use them to build your understanding of the federal government's operations, and make the choice to play a constructive role in securing the nation.

Larry C. Johnson
CEO, BERG Associates, LLC
Washington, D.C.

1

The Aftermath of September 11, 2001

The catastrophic events of September 11, 2001, served as a serious reminder to all Americans as to just how vulnerable everyday life had become in the twenty-first century. The United States watched in horror while, on a clear, blue-skied morning, hijacked commercial airliners laid waste to the Twin Towers of New York City's World Trade Center complex and to an entire wing of the Pentagon. The major media networks made this apocalyptic disaster painfully clear in excruciating real-time detail to stunned, if not traumatized, American and global audiences; the viewing public was then subjected to daily reruns of the tragedy for months to follow.

The leadership of U.S. President George W. Bush, New York City Mayor Rudy Giuliani, and others prevented a national panic. They quickly established a foundation of strength and stability from which the nation could recover from the immediate terror and confusion of the first-response and rescue operations.

In the minutes that followed the realization that the United States had been deliberately and savagely attacked by a cruel and unknown enemy, the nation's international transportation system ground to a halt. In the interest of national safety and security, no one was allowed to move about freely until the nature and size of the attacking force were known. Air traffic was immediately grounded, for the airways had provided the initial avenue of attack. Seaports were also closed immediately, due to their vulnerability to further attacks. U.S. Coast Guard vessels and personnel were assigned to patrol "high-value security areas" in ports and harbors. Sea marshals were assigned to escort or ride aboard commercial vessels entering and leaving various ports.

Why Don't They Like Us?

As the events of 9/11 unfolded and the horrific spectacles of the World Trade Center towers collapsing and part of the Pentagon crushed and on fire were displayed in real time for all the world to see, the questions of who perpetrated these acts of inhumanity and why they were so obviously directed at the United States became foremost in the minds and consciousness of the American people. The public soon realized that more than 120,000 terrorists, who had been trained in camps, had also gone largely unnoticed or even ignored by the leading governments of the world, most notably the United States. These terrorists were able to establish covert networks that threatened the safety, stability, and progress of the nations and people they targeted. This realization presented a dilemma that is as yet unsolved and that some observers feel never will be, given the social, political, and economic disparities that have been made so prevalent through the process of globalization. World leadership must be united in an effort to defeat terrorism by analyzing its root causes and implementing appropriate measures to guarantee that events like those of 9/11 will never happen again. This task is made difficult by the dominating global presence the United States has come to occupy and the resentment this has engendered in many parts of the world, especially in places where terrorism thrives. Thomas L. Friedman, the prize-winning journalist and author of "*Longitudes and Attitudes*," after a year of onsite Middle Eastern analysis, describes the core of terrorism in the region as being the result of exasperation on the part of young Arab men whose aspirations are frustrated by a lack of opportunity for advancement, especially in the oil-rich kingdoms where the polarization of wealth is constantly on display. This experience, when compared with the shining democratic and economic success of Israel, with its close ties to, if not dependency on, the United States, injures the dignity of devout Muslim youth and drives them into the arms of villainous terrorists such as Osama bin Laden, where they easily become indoctrinated in the ever-growing siege mentality against "fortress America." Even with the tremendous technological superiority enjoyed by the United States, time is always on the side of the terrorists with regard to opportunities for attack, and much remains to be done to eliminate the root causes of terrorism and thereby the threat it poses. World governments—with the active support of all of their citizens—must continue to take on this difficult task.

Shoreside entrances and exits to port and terminal facilities received added security assistance from National Guard forces and local law enforcement agencies. Rail and trucking traffic was severely curtailed until satisfactory threat analysis and cargo tracking and search procedures could be implemented.

ECONOMIC IMPACT

As the nation's transportation system was brought to a standstill in response to the perceived terrorist threat, it quickly became evident that the U.S. economy could not continue to perform at efficient levels if a regime of strict security controls were imposed. Manufacturing plants accustomed to "just in time" inventory sizing were forced to shut down production due to security-imposed slowdowns in the inbound supply chains. Aviation, particularly passenger service, did not operate fully in some airports for weeks. When flights did resume, they operated at a greatly decreased capacity that did not approach 50 percent of pre-9/11 levels until a year and a half later. Trucking was backed up at the Canadian and Mexican borders well into the winter of 2002–2003.

Rail traffic enjoyed an increase in ridership due to a fear of flying phenomenon, but it was initially plagued by a series of false bomb threats that caused the cancellation and rescheduling of many trains. As Americans became aware of the details surrounding the 9/11 tragedy, a bewildered but determined nation began to move forward in an effort to overcome its grief and to guarantee that a similar event would never again occur.

DOMESTIC REFORMS

While President Bush was sending U.S. forces and their coalition allies to attack terrorist strongholds in Afghanistan, Congress set to work to establish domestic security reforms that attempted to provide the means to successfully detect and prevent any future terrorist attacks. In October 2001, Congress passed the Transportation Security Act. This law provided immediate reforms in aviation security and required that additional legislation and programs be established in the maritime and port security arena.

Two years prior to the 9/11 attacks, President Bill Clinton had commissioned a group of seaport security experts to begin an analysis of crime and conspiracies that posed threats to the people and critical infrastructures of seaport cities. The Clinton Port Security Commission was established on April 27, 1999. After a year-long period of port visits and security analysis, the commission reported that there were no standard security policies and procedures among U.S. ports. In addition, the various law enforcement and related intelligence communities serving the waterfront operated so independently of one another that criminal elements were able to take advantage of these organizational gaps and effectively engage in criminal activity all along U.S. seacoasts.

The commission produced a report that included a set of twenty findings and recommendations. If these recommendations had been correctly understood and implemented, they would have solved many of the port security problems and weaknesses discovered in the national security self-examination period that was part of the aftermath of September 11, 2001.

Still, the Clinton Port Security Commission findings had resulted in congressional action prior to the September 2001 terrorist attack. Senator Fritz Hollings, the Democratic Transportation Committee chairman, had introduced legislation in April 2001 to respond to the findings of the Clinton Port Security Commission. The bill, called "S1412," was cosponsored by Senator Bob Graham, whose home state of Florida figured prominently in the planning of any federal port and maritime security program. With five major container-vessel and passenger-vessel ports, Florida was ahead of other states in their maritime security. In January 2001, the state had passed a rigorous code for port and maritime security that had become a standard for how to combat the waterfront criminal element.

INTERNATIONAL MARITIME REFORMS

Another element that was developing prior to the events of 9/11 was the International Standards Organization (ISO) global advocacy of international maritime standards. The International Maritime Organization (IMO), a sub-organization of the United Nations (UN) composed of more than 200 member countries, had implemented a program of standards of training and certification for mariners. Developed during the 1990s and in keeping with IMO policy, this program was designed to create a baseline of maritime safety for everyone employed on vessels of specified tonnage sailing on international voyages.

The IMO was approached by a U.S. Coast Guard (USCG) delegation in January 2002 with a written recommendation for the "Prevention and Suppression of Acts of Terrorism against Shipping." This document, carefully prescribed by USCG security experts, called for a number of provisions to be adopted by the IMO at its December 2002 annual meeting in London. These provisions would have a profound impact on the safety of maritime personnel on ships in port and at sea, shoreside in ports, along waterfronts, and at commercial maritime terminals and intermodal facilities. In its proposal, the USCG also recommended the implementation of international automatic identification systems and emergency signaling systems for ships.

CONTAINER SECURITY

The U.S. Customs Service was very busy during the period of recovery and reaction after the events of September 11, 2001. The Customs Service had developed and begun putting in place the Container Security Initiative, which involved the inspection (at the ports of origin) of cargo containers bound for U.S. ports. The requirement for screening of containerized cargo was the result of intelligence that indicated that terrorists might ship hidden explosive devices or other weapons of mass destruction inside the twenty-to-forty-foot metal-sealed cargo containers. The twenty largest container ports in the world, which together handle 90 percent of containerized cargo, were organized into a cooperative arrangement whereby U.S. Customs representatives performed on-site inspections of designated high interest containers. The representatives analyzed the cargo to determine which containers may be of a high-threat nature. Foreign ports also wanted to participate in this cooperative program, because they didn't want to lose their competitive position in the global economy.

The U.S. Customs Service Container Security Initiative addressed one of the very reasons why the 9/11 attack was able to be carried out so easily by the terrorists—namely, the powerful U.S. economy. Driven by free-market principles, the economy would surface again—only this time in support of the counter-measures employed against future terrorist acts.

CARGO SAFETY

Another quickly developing maritime security program involving global cooperation among major ports was Operation Safe Cargo. This program combined governmental elements of the Department of Transportation, including the U.S. Coast Guard, the Federal Highway Administration and the Volpe Transportation Center, the U.S. Customs Service, the U.S. Immigration and Naturalization Service, the U.S. ports of New York–New Jersey, Los Angeles, Long Beach, and Seattle-Tacoma, and various state and regional planning organizations relating to those ports, the European ports of Rotterdam and Hamburg, and the Pacific port of Singapore, along with several major commercial maritime companies that operate ships and port facilities.

The objectives of Operation Safe Cargo were threefold. They included the expansion of cargo security into the port of origin instead of only at the port of arrival, the advocacy of cutting-edge technology to monitor the content and movement of cargo in transit, and improved communication and cooperation among the federal and international agencies involved in the development of personnel and cargo security strategies and initiatives.

The driving force behind the establishment of Operation Safe Cargo was interest on the part of the security community in determining how existing transportation and logistics procedures could contribute to various terrorist threats, which included weapons of mass destruction that could be used in chemical, biological, or radiological forms and shipped as cargo; the use of legitimate hazardous cargo as a weapon, either on a ship or transported ashore; attacks on passenger vessels that could result in mass casualties; explosive detonations on vessels that could result in the closing of critical areas of the U.S. transportation network; attacks on aviation targets using shoulder-launched missiles from vessels nearby in ports; and waterborne attacks on critical public and commercial facilities using vessels as weapons. These concerns quickly emerged in the aftermath of 9/11 with the newly discovered knowledge that a global organization of well-trained terrorists whose leader had owned a fleet of ships and understood the business of shipping could attack anywhere at any time without notice, generating catastrophes similar to those suffered at the World Trade Center and the Pentagon.

Operation Safe Cargo was welcomed by security experts at the time of its introduction. It offered a comprehensive security package that included the appropriate transportation and government players, as well as the most effective security countermeasures aimed at the most critical security threats.

FUNDING SECURITY

Ambitious programs such as Operation Safe Cargo require substantial funding. Initially, "start-up" funding was supplied by most of the participating organizations at little cost. Additional funding mandated federally on a supplemental basis was to provide a strong financial structure for the completion of its many initiatives by mid-2002.

In February 2002, Congress created a Port Security Grants program to address funding for the extra security precautions required in the war against terrorism. This program was to be administered through the Department of Transportation via the new Transportation Security Agency, with support from the U.S. Coast Guard and the Maritime Administration. In July 2002, $93 million for port security assessments and equipment was awarded to those ports that had applied and submitted what experts at the U.S. Coast Guard and the Maritime Administration regarded as appropriate plans for port security analysis and upgrade. The Transportation Security Agency (TSA) needed the help of the U.S. Coast Guard and the Maritime Administration in analyzing the grant requests from the ports; the Land and Maritime Department in the TSA had only a director and a few staff members appointed, since it was a brand-new agency.

The majority of the grant money was awarded to ports in states such as Florida, which already had landmark maritime security legislation in place and was moving rapidly in the right direction. Other ports that had not been through an assessment program and had less clearly defined security programs did not fare as well with the funding awards. Many were required to wait for the second round of grants that was scheduled to be announced in December 2002.

CUSTOMS-TRADE PARTNERSHIP

In addition to its role in developing the Cargo Security Initiative, the U.S. Customs Service produced the Custom-Trade Partnership against Terrorism (C-TPAT). This was a joint initiative between government and business designed to protect the security of cargo entering U.S. ports and maintain a smooth and economically efficient flow of trade. If terrorists could interrupt the flow of trade by creating so much fear and anxiety that free and open market principles would be sacrificed in favor of a system of heavy security inspection and regulation, they would have succeeded in slowing the progress of democratic and advanced economic countries of the world.

In order to promote the free flow of trade in ports and other transportation hubs, the U.S. Customs Service offered "fast lanes" to shippers and transporters who took steps to secure their cargo against terrorist practices. C-TPAT was launched in April 2002 and required importers to "assess, evolve, and communicate new practices" that would improve the level of security throughout their entire supply chain. In return for this extra security analysis at each step of the transportation process, the U.S. Customs Service provides "fast lane," or expedited, security processing of cargo through the ports and borders it regulates.

The C-TPAT program was modeled on an earlier U.S. Customs Service maritime industry outreach program from the 1990s, called the "Sea Carrier Initiative." The Sea Carrier Initiative was, among other things, instrumental in the war against drugs. C-TPAT promises support rather than punishment for mariners who cooperate in maritime narcotics investigations. With C-TPAT, participating businesses must agree to assess their security systems according to U.S. Customs Service guidelines, complete a security questionnaire for submission to the U.S. Customs Service, implement new security programs per U.S. Customs Service guidelines, and agree to promote C-TPAT policy to other companies in the supply chain. Many large corporate entities, such as General Motors, Ford, Daimler Chrysler, Motorola, and Target, have rushed to sign on in order to enhance or maintain their competitive advantage and to help in the war against terrorism.

MARITIME SAFETY BECOMES A PRIORITY
In the closing months of 2002, a whirlwind of maritime security policies and procedures, both federal and international, came into being. With some variance on a few specific and important issues, these policies and procedures generally represented the culmination of a consensus maritime security program. This program should prove to be both efficient with regard to economic flow of cargo and passengers and effective in providing the appropriate countermeasures for safety against terrorism.

The Maritime Transportation Security Act, formerly known as S1214, passed through the Senate-House conference and was signed into law in late November 2002 by President George W. Bush. The Maritime Transportation Security Act had many provisions based not only on events related to September 11, 2001, but also on the findings of the Clinton Port Security Commission. Specific security requirements for ports, including standard security assessments with related security plan development and well-defined physical security requirement specifications, were highlighted in the act, with precise required dates of implementation.

A month later, in December 2002, the International Maritime Organization's Maritime Safety Council met and passed recommendations for the International Shipping and Port Security Check Codes that incorporated the U.S. Coast Guard suggestions of a year earlier. The international community had acted expeditiously and embraced the U.S. maritime security program in its entirety. As a result, changes could be affected globally among international security organizations such as the World Customs Organization, the International Chamber of Shipping, and the International Association of Ports and Harbours, to name a few. A true consensus on global maritime security policies and procedures had come about, and the atmosphere in which terrorism and maritime crime had previously flourished was about to undergo a massive sea change.

The chapters that follow will examine in detail the development of the programs that were created primarily in response to the events of September 11, 2001, although many of the concepts had been moving forward (albeit with much less energy) prior to that date. Throughout history, significant events have caused significant change, and in maritime security, the events of 9/11 have driven significant improvement. What remains to be done and who will bear the required costs will be issues that will demand continuous attention for many years. The immediate burst of momentum generated by the tragic events of 9/11 and the initial energy must not be allowed to dissipate.

2

History of
Maritime Security

Throughout maritime history, maintaining security onboard vessels at sea and in port along waterfronts has been an ongoing challenge. From Blackbeard's days as the world's most infamous pirate, preying on the Spanish galleons and then fleeing to his Caribbean hideouts, through the menacing acts of hijacking and ransom practiced by the Barbary Coast pirates, to the "hit and run" practices of today's Straits of Malacca pirates, the maritime environment has always been rife with opportunity for criminals to perform acts of violence and other crimes on the seas.

The primary difficulties in the maintenance of an effective maritime security program are the sheer size of the ocean and the formidable magnitude of its coastline and estuaries. When social, economic, and political divisions are added to this environment, the ability of nations to agree on cooperative solutions to maritime security can be overwhelming. The maritime nations of the world have historically assumed the responsibility for maintaining a semblance of ocean security through their navies to support commerce for reasons of trade and political and social stability. Throughout history, the Spanish, British, French, Dutch, Portuguese, German, and most recently, U.S. navies have been the foundation of maritime security in their respective geographical spheres of influence. These naval powers have been in conflict at times, and maritime security and the associated vulnerability of vessels at sea has suffered accordingly. Whenever a global naval power's strength has been weakened, either through conflict or political or economic collapse, local maritime criminal activity has taken advantage of the geographic security vacuum. During these times, the criminal elements have enjoyed relative freedom in pursuing piracy, hijacking, and smuggling operations.

As the European colonial powers gradually withdrew from their various global dominions, they more often than not left behind precarious and unstable maritime security situations. These situations resulted in the growth of the crime-infested coastal waters of South America, Africa, and the Middle East, as well as much of the Pacific and Indian oceans—areas in which maritime crime persists today. The emerging former colonial areas typically did not have the ability to establish strong maritime security programs until a stable shoreside infrastructure had been put into place. In some coastal regions, the development of stable governments is yet a work in progress. Until greater resources and the required political support are available in these areas, there will be a serious flaw in the fight against maritime criminal activity. These flaws will provide fertile areas for the growth and continued existence of today's terrorist groups, which can utilize the maritime resources at their disposal.

THE RESPONSIBILITY OF MARITIME DEFENSE

From a shipboard or seaside perspective, the earliest attempts at self-defense against maritime marauders involved arming the crew and defending the ship to the last man. Regardless of the port state's ability to maintain coastal and port security, shipowners and vessel operators considered the defense of the ship and the safety of the cargo to be the responsibility of the shipmaster and crew. A life at sea was deemed to be the realm of only the heartiest people, and therefore, the safety of the ship, crew, and cargo would presumably be preserved over time. The validity of this concept was often successfully challenged by the criminal element, to the detriment of both maritime personnel and business interests.

Maritime history is full of examples in which the value of a vessel's cargo was more than enough to offset the risk of capture and punishment—particularly when the ocean environment provided such an unlimited potential for a successful getaway. At the beginning of the twentieth century, reform within the maritime community put an emphasis on the welfare and safety of the seafarer. The responsibility for defending the ship and cargo against maritime crime became an obligation of the operating company or flag state navy rather than a job for the ship's crew. Crew members were forbidden to have weapons on board to protect themselves, and most commercial ships discontinued the practice of maintaining any type of defensive capabilities.

THE MARITIME INDUSTRY MATURES

As the global maritime industry continued to mature, shipboard operations evolved that further increased the vulnerability of vessels attacked at sea. While the size and speed of merchant vessels grew tremendously, which made it more difficult to catch and climb aboard cargo and passenger ships at sea, the size of crews steadily decreased as technological advancement in shipboard and cargo terminal equipment operations caused organizational downsizing. In addition, the economic cost considerations related to the interaction of vessel operating company management with powerful maritime unions dedicated to increasing the safety and living standards of their mariner membership also provided downward pressure on the size of vessel crews. This trend made it much easier for stowaways and other illegal boarders to come on surreptitiously and remain hidden. The smaller size of the crew also diminished the advantage of the shipboard personnel in any physical confrontation with attackers, although the element of surprise and a few weapons had often been sufficient in the past to commandeer a typical commercial vessel.

Cost considerations necessary for the profitable operation of commercial shipping worked against the funding required for effective security programs both in port and at sea. In the highly competitive business of global commercial shipping, all costs must be justifiable and demonstrate a value added to product or service and a verifiable return on an investment. When developing an effective shipboard security program, the tests of value added and return on investment are difficult to quantify. Often they are the considerations emphasized least in the determination of ship operating and overhead costs.

MEDIA ATTENTION DRIVES INTERNATIONAL AWARENESS

Two significant maritime events that demonstrated the vulnerability of ships at sea and caught the attention of the world through close media coverage were the hijackings of the *Santa Maria* and the *Achille Lauro*. Although these events happened nearly twenty-five years apart, there were similarities between them that underscored the ease with which a determined criminal could take control of a ship at sea.

The *Santa Maria* was a Portuguese-owned cruise vessel with 600 passengers and a crew of 300 that sailed to Port Everglades, Florida, en route from Venezuela. In January 1961, a group of twenty South American terrorists, who were aboard posing as passengers, captured the cruise ship. The terrorists, who were part of the Iberian Revolutionary Leadership Liberation Group, planned to sail the vessel to Africa and attack colonial provinces that they felt should contribute to the overthrow of the Salazar and Franco regimes in Portugal and Spain. Shipping authorities discovered the missing *Santa Maria* when the vessel stopped in St. Lucia to offload injured passengers. Upon discovery, the terrorist leader, Captain Galvao, surrendered to a U.S. Navy destroyer that was carrying a very interested international press corps. The *Santa Maria* was escorted safely to Recife, Brazil, in order to resume normal operations. The terrorists were taken into custody, and the press ensured that the world knew the painful and embarrassing details of the hijacking.

The *Achille Lauro* was hijacked in October 1985 en route to Israel by a group of Palestine Liberation Organization (PLO) terrorists in the Mediterranean Sea. The terrorists' plan was to enter port, capture the vessel, and demand the release of fifty of their colleagues, who were being held in prison in Israel. A crew member discovered the terrorists and their weapons, and the PLO hijackers were forced to capture the *Achille Lauro* prematurely and abort their original plan. A 69-year-old handicapped Jewish passenger named Leon Klinghoffer was killed when the terrorists took over the vessel. His body and his wheelchair were thrown overboard. The hijackers surrendered to Egyptian forces in return for safe passage home. The Egyptian aircraft transporting the terrorists was then forced to land in Sicily by U.S. fighter planes, but the Italian government released the terrorists a short time later. This incident was yet another maritime catastrophe that was closely watched by the media but, tangled in the mire of international politics, it had a less than a desirable outcome.

DEFENSE AGAINST PIRACY AND HIJACKING

In general, during the late twentieth century, the most probable threat to shipping at sea was a pirate attack or cargo hijacking. These situations usually occurred in commercially and politically emerging areas of the world where there were few or no maritime security forces to deter criminals. Cargo hijacking, stowaways, and smuggling were commonplace along the South American and African coasts. At certain locations in the South China Sea and Straits of Malacca, incidents of piracy were reported several times a week.

With an increasing number of larger and faster ships plying the commercial trade routes, the practice of making a vessel an unattractive target became the most successful mode of shipboard self-defense against pirates. Ships that employed piracy countermeasures and were trained in threat awareness were less apt to be singled out for attack. Those vessels that demonstrated readiness, vigilance, and a willingness to react to pirates were generally left alone, compared to the vessels that took little precaution. The careful use of lighting, stationing of extra lookouts, good housekeeping with respect to locked ship accessways, and of course, constant vigilance in high-threat areas, were usually sufficient to cause pirates to look elsewhere for an easier vessel to board.

THE NEED FOR INTERNATIONAL MARITIME SECURITY

During the second half of the twentieth century, several maritime conferences were held to discuss what constituted an act of piracy with regard to national and international waters, what the difference was between terrorism and piracy, what were the rights of stowaways and criminals, and who held the liability and responsibility for acts of violence that took place at sea. The leading nations of the world had realized that maritime crime was a serious issue that ultimately affected all of humanity, either directly or indirectly. Through the sponsorship of the United Nations Convention on the Law of the Sea, initiatives were defined for improved maritime security and nations agreed to support these initiatives continuously. Although people were committing many acts of maritime crime on a regular basis, it was felt that most commercial vessels would be able to complete their voyages safely if they simply took some precaution. The nations involved agreed that vessels should maintain an appropriate level of shipboard awareness, preparation, and training to successfully avoid the risk of attack. In addition, they stated that they believed maritime threats on the high seas were being contained within acceptable levels.

The increase in trade based on the growth of containerization and the expanding global economy of the late 1990s had ocean trade routes surging with shipping. For the first time in two decades, there were often more jobs worldwide than there were mariners to fill them. Shipping was on the rise and the establishment of the International Maritime Bureau's Office of Piracy Prevention in Kuala Lumpur (the capital of Malaysia) in December 1991 provided a valuable asset in combating and quantifying criminal maritime activity. It also fostered a global media focus on the plight of the mariner; before this time, piracy threats were little known to the general public.

MARITIME CRIMES FAIL TO GENERATE PUBLIC CONCERN

Unlike commercial aviation, which has had a highly publicized record of hijackings, piracy, and terror, maritime incidents have typically occurred far outside the public view. Historically, the industry has had little success in generating popular concern for maritime crime or violence at sea. An event that illustrates this general lack of worry about the plight of a globally effective maritime security program occurred in August 2000 in the Mediterranean Sea. A commercial ship, the *Delaware Bay*, was stopped and boarded off the coast of Montenegro by a patrol craft operated by a group of Serbian commandos. The U.S.-flagged *Delaware Bay* was on a voyage to deliver grain and humanitarian supplies to refugees in the former Republic of Yugoslavia. However, the Serbian commandos believed the vessel had delivered weapons to Albania and vowed to arrest the captain, ship, and crew as enemies of their state. The commando leader told the captain of the *Delaware Bay* to destroy his emergency signaling equipment and to sail his vessel to a nearby naval base for arrest. Luckily, the quick-witted veteran skipper of the *Delaware Bay* was able to convince the commandos of his innocence by reconstructing his voyage and providing them with a little ransom money for their cause.

This event transpired over the course of two days with little or no government intervention or rescue, because of the delicate balance of international political events in the area at that time. The shipping company and maritime industry representatives were furious that the *Delaware Bay* was "hung out to dry." They insisted that if it had been a commercial airliner, appropriate government agencies and rescue teams would have been dispatched immediately to set the aircraft, crew, and passengers free.

Throughout the ages, the shipping industry has enjoyed relative anonymity from public scrutiny. It has prospered from loose oversight and lack of governmental control. The unfortunate downside to this freedom is a lack of awareness and media attention during maritime emergencies, as was the case with the *Delaware Bay*, when not enough was known to effectively react to the threat.

MARITIME TERRORISM

Prior to the events of September 11, 2001, both maritime industry and security experts considered the main threats to commercial shipping to be an unlikely piracy, stowaway, or smuggling event in an unstable area where lack of preparation or awareness on the part of the vessel or its operating company would be the contributing factor. They thought that terrorist attacks would most likely occur in commercial aviation, as aviation presented seemingly easier targets for attack with much higher media exposure. Public concern over an aviation attack could produce a political impact that an act of piracy probably could not.

The devastating suicide bombing attack delivered by Al Qaeda terrorists on the U.S.S. *Cole*, a U.S. Navy frigate refueling pierside in Yemen in October 2000, served as a warning that events were afoot that could and would alter the course of not only maritime but global history as well. The analysis of the *Cole* incident was in its final stages when the 9/11 attacks on the World Trade Center and Pentagon took place. The relationship between these incidents and the conclusions that can be drawn from them will continue to be of profound interest to the international security community as it attempts to combat global terrorism and guard against the possibility of similar events occurring in the future.

In the aftermath of the 9/11 events, a plan to attack a U.S. Navy aircraft carrier battle group in Singapore was discovered and almost carried out, but it was ultimately foiled by excellent international intelligence and police work. The intelligence also brought to light the fact that Osama bin Laden, the leader of the terrorist Al Qaeda movement, had close ties to the shipping industry and at one time had owned a fleet of commercial vessels.

In December 2002, the terrorist community struck a blow squarely in the face of the commercial maritime industry by exploding a French-owned supertanker, the *Limberg*, as it entered port in Yemen. The bombing not only caused an immediate environmental disaster and temporarily compromised

The Bin Laden Shipping Company

Shortly after the events of 9/11, as authorities were trying to put the loose investigative pieces of the Al Qaeda puzzle together, it was discovered that the chief terrorist himself, Osama bin Laden, had interests in shipping and may have owned as many as twenty-three ships at one time. Only months later, a bin Laden family member was discovered in an Italian port, hidden inside a customized intermodal container en route from Turkey to Spain. The container was air-conditioned and had eating, sleeping, and bathroom facilities.

The tendency of national governments to leave the various operating elements of the maritime industry to their own devices and limit governmental oversight of maritime affairs has contributed to a legacy of mystery and corruption. The fact that shipping industry operations involve large capital investments, are generally considered critical to the security and economic success of a nation, and—until recently—involved only a few major wealthy players with special political connections, also contributed to this legacy. Shipping "conferences," which for a long time were an industry practice that fixed freight rates among consenting major shipping companies in a cartel-like manner, along with fractious relationships between the different shipping unions and company management, and the type of fierce, if not ruthless, leadership that is required to succeed all combine to create a rugged business environment that is unfriendly and unfamiliar to government regulation. The Hollywood film *On the Waterfront*, which featured Marlon Brando, Lee J. Cobb, and Rod Steiger playing thugs and hoodlums portrayed the worst of the maritime scenario in its telling story of union and shipping company racketeering on the New York City shore. Maritime security and law enforcement personnel are up against a formidable challenge, not only due to the modern complexity of the cargo operation and document administration, but more importantly, to a long-standing legacy of graft and corruption.

the French government's diplomatic efforts toward conciliation in the Middle East, but, most significantly, it served notice to the commercial maritime industry that it was no longer exempt from terrorist attacks, and those attacks could take place anywhere.

3

Maritime Security Implementation

Although the prevalence of criminal acts has been evident throughout the development of the global maritime industry, dominant forces within the industry (insurers, owners, and operators) have long believed that, as in any other business endeavor, they had to assume some level of risk. They considered the observed or reported level of criminal activity to be generally acceptable—until September 11, 2001. The cost of staying competitive at a global level simply did not allow for the expense of zero-tolerance maritime security programs. Substantial study and analysis regarding the development and successful establishment of these types of programs had occurred in the latter stages of the twentieth century and had gained the support of many maritime groups concerned with worldwide safety and security standards, but these programs were cost-prohibitive.

After years of serious discussion, maritime security experts reached a consensus on the proper approach to guarding against perceived maritime threats and minimizing the effects of maritime crime both at sea and in port. These threats included cargo theft, piracy, terrorism, smuggling, and stowaways.

THE SECURITY SURVEY

The currently accepted approach toward building an effective security program is to begin with a thorough and accurate security survey or assessment that analyzes the hazards and threats faced by a particular ship or port. Based on the survey results, experts then develop (or redevelop) a detailed security plan to prevent or to serve as a countermeasure to any criminal activity of sufficient probability for concern. An outside source should perform the security survey, to ensure that it is conducted in an objective and organizationally impartial manner for effectiveness. In addition to creating detailed preventive and countermeasure procedures, the security plan must also emphasize regular training and intelligence gathering to promote the proper level of awareness for all those who will be involved when the plan is put into effect.

At a minimum, proper security survey procedure requires an analysis of current operating company organization, existing security personnel, previous security survey information (with regard to discrepancies and recommendations), and a careful examination, using related intelligence, of all potential threats. A description and analysis of the physical layout of the ship or facility is also critical to the security survey. The vessel or port must include an access schematic showing all possible entry and exit points, details regarding perimeter security (including fencing and surveillance), alarm devices and lighting locations, and type of coverage. The security survey must examine existing security assets, both internal to the ship or facility and external to local, state, and federal security elements.

Weapons of self-defense, which would include firearms (if allowed), should be inventoried as part of the survey with an emphasis on appropriate quantity, type, proper access, and stowage. Facilities or vessels that contain high value assets or have control areas that are critical to operations should be designated as security areas. Special attention should be given to these areas and access to them should be restricted.

The security survey should ensure that standard operating

procedures are in place or established for all ship or facility security-related events. These events include cargo movement, loading and discharge, and all personnel entrance and egress. The procedures should detail standard operations for ships in vulnerable circumstances, such as the procedure for ships entering and leaving port, when the vessel is burdened with slow speed and lack of maneuverability and is thus at greater risk of attack. The standard operating procedures should ideally utilize all ship or facility personnel. They should also be incorporated into a security bill that assigns stations and responsibilities for all operational events.

In addition to the operational procedures, a solid administrative program to support security training and drills needs to be an integral part of the security survey. All personnel should have background checks to verify their credentials. Following these checks, personnel should be issued identification cards, which will be a key element in the security administration program. To ensure secure facilities management, the access procedures for all personnel must be scrutinized at all ports. Because maritime port facilities have continuous inbound and outbound traffic, both shoreside and seaside, verification of personnel is difficult but necessary. An accurate and comprehensive security survey must include close analysis of the personnel and a passenger and baggage admittance process to maintain an effective security perimeter for safe and successful facility and ship operations.

Another component to consider in the security of port terminal facilities is that they are generally composed of multiple elements and adjacent to large cities. Also, they are geographically fixed and usually haven't been planned or built with appropriate consideration for security issues. Typically, seaport terminal facilities involve truck and rail intermodal components, as well as the pierside vessel cargo discharge process. Often, an in-depth approach to security defense is taken with increased levels of security imposed as proximity to the cargo piers is gained. For optimal safety and consequence management during heightened security conditions, a crisis management team concept is usually employed in port and terminal facilities. The team approach typically involves union, management, and government representatives across all the utilized modes of transportation during the security surveying and planning process. This is not to imply that shipboard security is any easier to maintain than shoreside security; rather, the gangway watch aboard vessels is singly most important to maintaining an effective security envelope about the ship. A scarcity of adequate security assets and personnel may hamper the successful management of shipboard security and this can usually be traced back to cost considerations.

THE SECURITY PLAN

Once the ship or facility security survey has been completed and reviewed by the requisite management authorities, it is used to develop a comprehensive security plan. The security plan should contain named and competent personnel who will be responsible for implementing and maintaining the program. These clearly identified personnel, such as the ship and facility security officers, should be at a high level (if not the highest level) of management to ensure that the security program will not be compromised. The security plan will also contain the necessary standard operating procedures for the operation or mission of the facility or vessel in question. Security bills should be developed to further delineate specific personnel responsibilities supporting the standard operating procedures.

A well-developed and successfully implemented and maintained security program is an achievement worthy of high praise. It must be supported by continuous awareness, vigilance, and training to reinforce the concepts fundamental to the security survey and plan. It must also be noted that an effective security program is expensive. It obviously requires many procedures that could be ignored if there were no criminal hazards or threats.

MARITIME SECURITY OBJECTIVES

The mission of the maritime industry is to provide transport for global and domestic commerce efficiently, as demonstrated by profit for ownership. However, the profit for ownership must now be tempered by the security required to keep maritime businesses and personnel safe. The costs of successful maritime security management in the aftermath of 9/11 have risen drastically due to the increased threat from terrorist groups. Terrorist threats demand additional and more expensive security equipment, as well as more and better-trained personnel to perform security missions successfully. At the same time, the efficient flow of maritime commerce has been slowed, through greater regulation and scrutiny. The increase in regulation and scrutiny is a direct result of new and emerging security risks made most evident by the terrorist attacks of 9/11 and related events that preceded and followed that horrific day. The objective of a successful maritime and port security program is to provide a protected environment from all perceived threats to the general safety and welfare of maritime personnel, vessels, and facilities. At the same time, the program should create minimal restriction to a healthy and prosperous trade in commerce.

The smooth flow of trade is the key to a successful global and domestic economy. It is also the key to the related freedom and success that today's progressing world so desperately needs. If terrorist acts result in the imposition of restrictions to trade caused by the overzealous implementation of security measures, then the terrorists have been successful in their attacks on the global economy and have effectively blocked our progress. In order to avoid this situational paralysis and achieve a safe and secure yet free-flowing and prosperous global trade system, a balance between effective security and efficient commerce must be reached. This balance can and must be achieved. However, years of neglect with regard to developing and maintaining security programs makes this process a serious challenge. Also contributing to the problem is a general lack of interest in the details of the global transportation system by both the governments and citizens of the world. All of these inherent difficulties have increased exponentially with the knowledge we acquired on 9/11—that terrorists could successfully conduct acts of mayhem on a massive scale.

UNDERSTANDING THE SECURITY THREATS

From the events of that catastrophic day and the best intelligence analysis currently available, a new awareness of the increase in potential threat magnitude and scope has energized the security world and its thinking. The maritime and port threat spectrum has been expanded to include twenty-to-forty-foot-long closed cargo containers that are shipped as freight. These containers could hide weapons of mass destruction, including chemical, biological, and nuclear devices, which could be detonated anywhere and at any time by atomic explosions or dirty bombs. (Dirty bombs consist of chemical, biological, or nuclear fragments that are detonated with conventional explosives and spewed over a large area.) Dry bulk cargo vessels carrying raw materials such as ores, coal, and minerals; construction materials, including cement, sand, and gravel; and scrap iron and grain have also been included on the list of potentially threatening elements. Each of these items provides an excellent "needle in a haystack" environment in which weapons of mass destruction might be hidden. In addition, wet bulk carriers, filled with petroleum or other refined chemical products, could be used just as the commercial jets were at the World Trade Center and the Pentagon. Terrorists could use the wet bulk carriers as weapons, burning and exploding surface torpedoes when correctly aimed or positioned.

Because most major ports are near large population centers and serve as critical hubs in a wider transportation network, a terrorist attack at a port could result in devastating damage. Not only might the attack produce high human casualty rates, but the use of a vessel as a weapon would also have a tremendous impact on global transportation.

Aside from using vessels themselves as weapons, there are many ways that terrorists might employ maritime resources in their attacks. For example, they could explode or sink ships in harbor entry channels, canals, and other restrictive areas. They could also hijack ships and then steer them into collisions with bridges or other pieces of critical shoreside infrastructure.

Although the cruise-line industry has an excellent safety and security track record, it will always be a target of interest to terrorists because of the high visibility and media exposure that would follow an attack on a major cruise liner.

MARITIME VESSELS AND CARGO

Also part of the new world threat awareness is a realization on the part of law enforcement and intelligence agencies that it is a complicated process to track both ship and cargo movement. Ships have always had an ability to disappear into a fog bank if necessary, and tracing the ownership of vessels is frequently a limitless event—almost like peeling an onion. With flags of convenience, offshore registries and banking, different levels and many different ways of operating, chartering, and brokering vessels, law enforcement officials and intelligence analysts are challenged to identify and locate potential terrorist activities on vessels and in ports. Those security personnel who haven't worked directly in the maritime industry, either shoreside or onboard a vessel, often find themselves puzzled by maritime mysteries and loopholes in their attempts to discover traceable records and locate

Port Shutdowns

An exercise sponsored by the Transportation Security Administration and produced and directed by the consulting firm Booz Allen Hamilton in October 2002 was designed to test the flexibility of the U.S. national transportation system and the impact a significant maritime security incident would have on the overall network. It had long been commonly felt among security experts that the maritime industry is extremely vulnerable to terrorist attacks, but the actual impact on the domestic economy had never been closely analyzed. The exercise began with a simulated truck accident at the Port of Los Angeles/Long Beach, which involved the discovery of a "dirty bomb"—fifty pounds of C-4 explosive surrounded by one hundred pounds of radioactive Cesium-137. In the exercise, on the same day as the Los Angeles incident, hypothetical suspected terrorists linked to Osama bin Laden were arrested in the Port of Savannah and a plot was discovered that caused the Customs Service to close all U.S. ports and borders. The result of the combined events was an accelerated economic disaster, with the stock market dropping five hundred points immediately. Cargo and manufacturing backlogs required several months to clear, and the total damage to the U.S. economy was estimated at $60 billion.

Ironically, the Port of New York and New Jersey was asked to take part in the exercise in place of the Port of Los Angeles/Long Beach, whose key personnel were involved in a longshoreman and dockworker strike—demonstrating in a real-time mode the true economic impact of a port closing. The entire West Coast was closed for several weeks, with devastating effects on the economy and the nation's transportation network.

Lessons learned from the exercise indicated that cargo screening needs to be conducted abroad at the port of origin, that individual organizational elements need standardized security systems, and that the government needs a national transportation security response plan that clearly defines the roles of all participants for better coordination.

accountable entities in commercial shipping. There are many exceptions and nuances in the global commercial freight transportation systems that have historically aided the use of subterfuge for competitive advantage. Cargo documentation is murky at best. The description "freight of any kind"—otherwise known as FAK—is common on shipping manifests and can be used to disguise many forms of cargo. "Bonded" cargo may be shipped to intermediate locations without proof of ownership declared and without clearing customs.

Transshipment is another process that creates difficulty in commercial cargo tracking, as cargo containers may be routed through hubs and then on via spokes to other destinations prior to their final arrival point. The port networks that constitute this hub-and-spoke cargo feeder system are part of the vast intermodal global transportation network, which includes trucking, rail, aviation, and maritime. Each mode of transportation is a culture unto itself, with its own method of doing business and its own ways of tracking and accounting for cargo. When consideration must also be made for all the different international borders and checkpoints that manufactured products must pass through, monitoring the whereabouts of any given shipment can become very complicated.

Identifying and locating cargo shipments that could be part of a terrorist conspiracy or attack is a difficult process that requires reliable intelligence and a thorough knowledge of the global intermodal transportation system. The key to success in searching for cargo threats is to identify anomalies in the transportation process. These anomalies may occur in the way a cargo container is stuffed or packed, the way the cargo manifest paper trail evolves, or the way the cargo is routed from its point of departure to the point of delivery. The global transportation network, and particularly its maritime mode, has traditionally operated with relative freedom from government regulation and scrutiny with respect to the cargo accounting process. Many improvements and much progress must therefore be made both domestically and internationally in order to reach a satisfactory level of transportation safety and security.

Port Security
Team Members

Throughout almost four centuries of U.S. maritime history, responsibility for port and maritime facility security has gradually come under the cognizance of state or local government entities called port authorities. Port authorities generally are part of the state or local government in which they reside. The port authority director and the associated port authority commissioners are appointed by and report to their respective state governors, legislatures, or local elected officials. The port authority police work closely with federal, state, and local law enforcement agencies to maintain safety and effective security on the waterfront and its shoreside accesses. The port authority police are responsible for criminal acts relating to all waterfront commerce and activity, while the U.S. Coast Guard maintains jurisdiction and control over all shipping that enters and leaves the various U.S. ports.

The U.S. Coast Guard was originally established as a federal agency in the U.S. Treasury Department in 1790 and was then transferred to the Department of Transportation in 1967. The Coast Guard is responsible for the general safety and security of the U.S. coastline and the U.S. flagged maritime shipping industry. The U.S. Coast Guard is the only federal government maritime entity with the legal authority to arrest ships at sea; it becomes part of the Department of Defense in times of war.

In addition to the port authority police and the Coast Guard, there are two other important divisions of the port security team. They are the U.S. Customs Service and the U.S. Immigration and Naturalization Service. The U.S. Customs Service has been a federal agency within the U.S. Treasury Department since its establishment in 1789. The Customs Service is responsible for guarding our nation against the influx of contraband, which includes all illegal cargo and narcotics. The U.S. Immigration and Naturalization Service has been a federal agency within the U.S. Justice Department since it was created in 1891, and it is responsible for keeping illegal aliens out of our country.

These traditional bodies are in a process of change. The U.S. Coast Guard, the U.S. Customs Service, and the U.S. Immigration and Naturalization Service are all moving under the banner of the newly formed U.S. Homeland Security Department. This department was officially established by the Homeland Security Act, passed by the 107th session of Congress in November 2002, at the request of the Bush administration, as part of the effort to improve U.S. security in the aftermath of September 11, 2001.

THE PORT AUTHORITY'S SECURITY RESPONSIBILITIES

The general mission of the port authority police, often called the port authority public safety department, is to "plan, develop, implement and administrate policies and programs, which provide for an effective police force and result in the suppression of crime, the preservation of law and order and the protection of life and property." This mission is an all-encompassing concept and a very large responsibility for any government entity. It requires close coordination with all port authority elements, so that the business of the port authority—smoothly flowing commerce—can be carried out in an efficient and cost-effective manner. At the same time, the port authority must provide a safe and protected environment for all customers, facilities, and personnel in areas under the jurisdiction of the port.

In order to effect the required level of security at all the port authority locations, certain strategic objectives must be met. Because the area that the port authority covers is diverse (entryways, exits, tunnels, and bridges are all managed by the port authority, whereas piers and terminals are leased by operating companies), the port authority must employ the appropriate security technology. This includes effective fencing and lighting, closed-circuit television, laser and other motion detection systems, as well as chemical sensors and radiation detectors to provide warning against illegal intruders or the presence of life-endangering substances in areas not regularly monitored by security personnel. Alarm systems must be in place to ensure that the related threat mitigation personnel are notified expeditiously of any issues of concern and that the general populace is made aware of any potential or actual danger.

Effective fencing is usually defined by security experts as being at least eight feet in height with an additional three feet of concertina wire (coiled barbed wire) slanted outward at a forty-five-degree angle. Proper lighting acts as a deterrent and is critical to the prevention of crime, as the vast majority of criminal events occur in darkness, which provides cover for both the staging and operation of illegal acts. When properly deployed, closed-circuit television and other sensor and detector systems can be more reliable and, in the long term, more cost-effective than maintaining a large force of security personnel.

The security sensor and detector systems should be integrated in a well-coordinated alarm system complete with effective communications. This integration ensures that the appropriate security personnel and first responders are alerted to any threat or criminal act that may be occurring. The cost of implementing and maintaining security systems with proven technology can be expensive. In some cases, the responsibility for funding is passed along to the terminal operators who lease port authority-owned areas for their commercial cargo and passenger operations.

The port authority must also provide training for its security personnel. They must deploy them in a balanced manner to deal optimally with any criminal threats or acts they may encounter. In order to do this successfully, a steady and reliable process of threat intelligence analysis and investigation must be ongoing. This analysis requires close cooperation with both domestic and international law enforcement agencies. Finally, the port authority must ensure that its safety and security personnel are ready to be mobilized expeditiously for mass emergencies. Being ready for such events implies a close working relationship with local law enforcement and public safety elements and requires a managerial dedication in support of the continuous improvement of police services and safety. Given the large amount of real estate and the limited budgets port authority police and safety departments must deal with, the stated goals and desired success of their security programs often fall short of expectations.

THE U.S. COAST GUARD'S SECURITY RESPONSIBILITIES

The port authority's primary partner on the port security team is the U.S. Coast Guard. Because this federal agency is designated to ensure the security of our ports, waterways, and maritime borders, it is responsible for guarding against seaward threats that may arrive via vessels of any type. The Coast Guard, which was set up shortly after independence and originally called the Revenue Cutter Service, has undergone many transformations. It probably has more missions—and less funding to effectively accomplish these missions—than any other federal agency. Nonetheless, the men and women of the Coast Guard valiantly perform their duties of protecting

Sea Marshals and Maritime Guardians

Keeping ships safe when they are in port can actually be more difficult than when they are at sea. Many ships get under way from their berths at piers to avoid being damaged by a storm because they will quite likely be able to escape or ride out a storm at sea. In the case of the U.S.S. *Cole*, the U.S. Navy frigate that was attacked in October 2000 from seaward by a small exploding craft while refueling pierside in Aden, Yemen, an area known to harbor terrorists, the threat was significant. To make matters worse, the *Cole*'s vulnerability was unable to be decreased since the vessel was immobile. In an effort to lessen the threat of terrorism, the U.S. Coast Guard has created a program whereby special detachments of sea marshals—armed active members of the Coast Guard, or reserve and auxiliary personnel—are used to board, investigate, and protect vessels as necessary. Increased vigilance and patrols are also part of Operation Liberty Shield, a U.S. Department of Homeland Security initiative designed to provide greater protection and safety for all major U.S. ports. This program is being enacted as a result of increased budget appropriations. Each inbound vessel is required to file a notice of arrival ninety-six hours in advance. The arrival notice must include crew and passenger lists for inspection by the Coast Guard. Cargo vessels are also required to submit cargo manifests for analysis twenty-four hours before the cargo is due to leave a port so that it can be analyzed by customs officials. Some commercial shipping companies have been utilizing the services of the legendary Gurkhas, the fiercely rugged knife-wielding servants and bodyguards of British Army officers. For about five hundred dollars per month, a team of five Gurkhas may be used to guard the gangway and other egress and exit areas onboard a ship in a port with inadequate security provisions. Another maritime security asset that mitigates the terrorist threat and diminishes shipboard vulnerability is the use of specially trained National Guard troops to provide additional protection and safety to crew members on Military Sealift Command (MSC) ships that are transiting high-threat or dangerous areas in the Southwest Asia and Persian Gulf areas. These Guardian Mariners, as they are called, provide an extra measure of security for MSC vessels, which deliver strategic equipment and supplies to U.S. armed forces overseas. These extra security measures can be expensive, but they are certainly cost-effective when viewed from the perspective of a worst-case terrorist scenario.

public security and safety from enemies of the United States while also taking care to preserve the global environment. They support safe maritime commercial operations both domestically and internationally with an organization of only 36,000 active duty personnel, supported by 8,000 reservists. Coast Guard duties include maritime drug interdiction as part of the National Drug Control Strategy, maritime search and rescue operations in support of ships at sea, homeland port security operations, and protection of natural resources and the environment from many forms of pollution.

The Coast Guard has its headquarters in Washington, D.C., and is divided into an Atlantic Area based in Portsmouth, Virginia, and a Pacific Area based in Alameda, California. The Atlantic and Pacific areas are broken into nine districts, each with a headquarters in a major port city region. The Coast Guard works to ensure security for U.S. ports, waterways, and maritime borders by focusing its strategy on "increased intelligence and information, controlled movement of high interest vessels, increased presence and response capabilities, improved critical infrastructure protection and greater inter-agency and international outreach." The Coast Guard is responsible for enforcing all maritime laws and treaties, and as a federal agency, it has the unique authority to board any vessel subject to U.S. jurisdiction to perform inspections, searches, inquiries and, if necessary, arrests. Interagency coop-eration and strong partnerships with international, state, and local governments are critical to the success of the Coast Guard's job.

The Coast Guard representative in a particular port area is the "Captain of the Port," who monitors and controls the movement of shipping into and out of the harbors. The Captain of the Port and representative elements are usually located at strategic areas in the port, so that the regulation of vessel movements can be performed as expeditiously and effectively as possible. The Captain of the Port uses a sophisticated high-tech Vessel Tracking System in major ports and shore-to-ship high frequency communications in smaller, less trafficked ports. All vessels greater than a specified tonnage are required to request permission to enter the harbor or inland traffic schemes per prescribed time limits through the Captain of the Port. The Captain of the Port enters the vessel's unique maritime mobile service identification number into the Coast Guard tracking and monitoring system. If the vessel is of high interest because of the type of cargo it may be carrying, the port it may have sailed from, or any other suspicious intelligence, the Captain of the Port or some higher authority may impose varying degrees of scrutiny on the vessel as necessary. The Captain of the Port has at his disposal a diverse mix of armed aviation and waterborne craft that can range from small high-speed patrol craft to large high-endurance cutters. Aircraft provide both short- and long-range surveillance and rescue capability.

U.S. CUSTOMS SERVICE'S SECURITY RESPONSIBILITIES

Another critical member of the port security team is the U.S. Customs Service. Its mission is to monitor and control all carriers, persons, and articles entering and leaving the United States. The Customs Service, established in 1789 to save the new nation from financial disaster by collecting duties on imports, has a long and varied history as a key government agency. On a daily basis, Customs Service personnel protect over 96,000 miles (154,497 kilometers) of U.S. land, air, and sea borders and more than 300 ports of entry—all with a total of only 20,000 employees. The Customs Service processes over $1 trillion in import trade each year and uses the latest in processing, analysis, and sensor equipment in order to effectively monitor commerce without impeding the flow of U.S. trade.

The Customs Service Automated Commercial Environment relies on specially designed importing data systems that are designed to lower the cost of trade compliance and administration and provide user-friendly service to the trade community. Authorities and experts in the global transportation sector have, for some time, been attempting to standardize the system used for cargo manifesting, accounting, and tracking so as to evolve from the cumbersome and complex (if not archaic) process in which each transporter or carrier has its own way of doing business. The Customs Service's goal is to create a paperless cargo clearance process that will also assist in targeting non-compliant cargo for further examination. The Customs Service Automated Manifest System provides shippers, customs brokers, customs agents, and law enforcement personnel with services including assessment and collection of fees, instant information on import quotas, and monitoring of high-risk shipments throughout the shipping process.

Customs agents also are skilled in the investigation of international money-laundering schemes. Laundering schemes are often the links between narcotics smuggling and the financing and trafficking of other illegal and dangerous cargos, including munitions, firearms, and weapons of mass destruction. Through the dedication of its workforce; technological innovation; its extensive air, land, and sea interdiction forces; and its capability, the Customs Service holds a key position in America's frontline against crime. Not only is its task critical, but it also provides the United States with a unique insight into the changing trends of global crime in commerce.

U.S. IMMIGRATION AND NATURALIZATION SERVICE'S SECURITY RESPONSIBILITIES

The last member of the port security team is the U.S. Immigration and Naturalization Service (INS). This agency administers U.S. immigration laws in 250 official ports of entry with air, land, and sea locations covering 36 districts—both domestic and abroad—with a staff of 30,000 employees. The INS has undergone substantial change since its initial establishment in 1891 as part of the Customs Service, under the authority of the Treasury Department. The Immigration Service, as it was called then, was responsible for collecting passenger lists from each incoming vessel, a process previously performed by the Customs Service. In the years that followed, the agency was transferred to the Department of Commerce and Labor in 1903, and then, in 1940, under the new name, the Immigration and Naturalization Service, it became part of the Department of Justice.

Given ongoing changes in world migration patterns; the ease of international travel for business, education, and tourism; and an increasing emphasis on controlling illegal immigration, the original organization of immigrant inspectors had evolved into a corps of officers focusing on "inspection, examination, adjudication, legalization, investigation, patrol and refugee asylum issues." Today, the INS continues to work with the Customs Service, using the Treasury Enforcement Communications System. Together, the two agencies perform instant checks on arrivals at land, sea, and air ports of entry and apprehend, remove, or deny entry to newcomers who have arrived illegally or aliens who have violated the regulations governing their stay.

The port security team—composed of the port authority, the U.S. Coast Guard and its Captain of the Port, the U.S. Customs Service, and the U.S. Immigration and Naturalization Service—is poised to ensure maritime security. These agencies provide shoreside security through the efforts of port authority police and through safety department security programs. They also ensure the seaside security of vessels, cargo, and passengers via the U.S. Coast Guard Captain of the Port Vessel Traffic Control System and the U.S. Customs Service

Automated Manifest System and their Treasury Enforcement Communications System, operated in cooperation with the Immigration and Naturalization Service. Commercial maritime shipping owners and their operating companies, brokers, and agents all conform to the port security team requirements by submitting ship operations plans, cargo manifest information, and passenger and crew lists. If they do not, they risk being denied entry to U.S. ports and their facilities.

5

Maritime Security Funding Process

The previous chapters provided information on the manner in which ships and ports operate, along with the concept of effective yet efficient security programs and their impact on the smooth flow of global trade. They also discussed in detail the diversity and magnitude of the maritime threat spectrum. This chapter includes the one remaining issue that is fundamental in the establishment of successful security programs: the funding process. Proper funding is vital in order to finance the development, implementation, and maintenance of security programs.

New federal and state security regulations and related legislation have emerged based on post-9/11 analyses. To meet these new requirements, U.S. ports are currently in desperate need of government financial assistance, and it appears that these financial woes will continue for the foreseeable future. Most of the coastal state governments in the period following 9/11 found themselves facing huge deficits that came about because of global and domestic economic declines. As a result, the states were not in a favorable position to contribute as much as they might have done otherwise to their various port security programs.

GOVERNMENTAL FUNDING PROCESS

The normal procedure for budgeting funds at the federal government level requires a two-year advanced planning process

The U.S.S. *Cole* is seen here in 1998 moving through the Persian Gulf on its way to support a military buildup in Southeast Asia. The *Cole* demonstrated the acute vulnerabilities of the maritime industry when it was bombed by terrorists in October 2000 while it was refueling in the port of Aden, Yemen.

A gaping hole is a reminder of the severe damage done to the *Cole* in the terrorist bombing that killed seventeen Americans. Although the *Cole* incident might have served as a warning to the U.S. government that terrorists were ready to exploit the nation's weaknesses, the country was still unprepared almost a year later when terrorists attacked the World Trade Center and Pentagon on September 11, 2001.

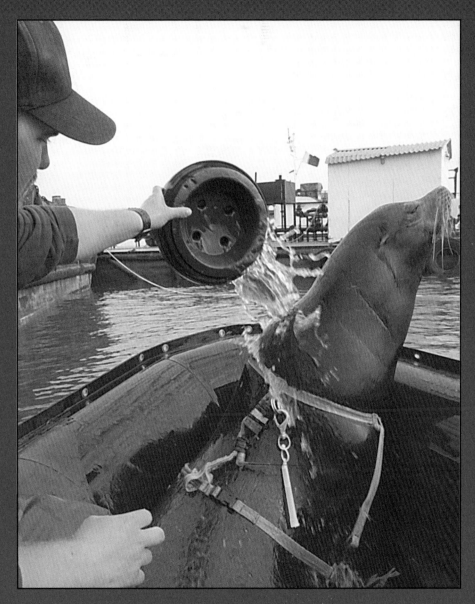

The U.S. Coast Guard is entrusted with many responsibilities, and it is often extremely understaffed. To help the Coast Guard with its maritime security duties, other members of the American armed forces—and even members of other species—may at times be called upon to help. The sea lion seen in this photograph has been specially trained to help the Coast Guard in particular missions.

When one hears the term "Customs Service," the image that is likely to spring to mind is one of a neatly uniformed official efficiently checking baggage and passports in an international airport. Most people don't realize that the duties of the U.S. Customs Service are often much more dangerous. These men are members of a Customs Service Special Response Team. They are engaging in a drill that will ensure that they are prepared if they ever have to physically overtake a suspicious vessel at the beachfront.

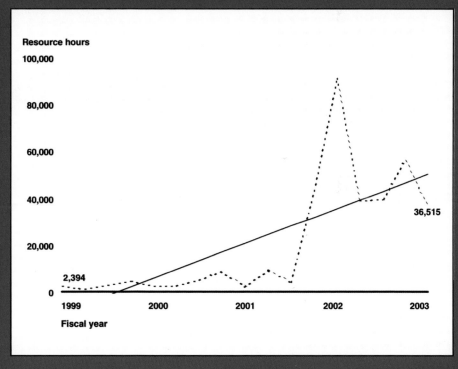

This graph, based on information provided by the U.S. General Accounting Office, shows the total number of hours devoted to maritime security—by cutters, boats, and aircraft—for the fiscal years 1999–2003. Although the time spent on port, waterway, and coastal safety spiked sharply in 2002 in the immediate wake of the September 11, 2001, attacks, the solid line demonstrates that the overall trend for the time period has been a somewhat more gradual increase.

MARITIME ADMINISTRATION BUDGET
(Dollars In Millions)

	2002 Actual	2003 1/ Request	2004 1/ Request
Maritime Security Program	99	99	99
Operations & Training	89	93	104
Ship Disposal	0	11	11
Maritime Guaranteed Loans	37	4	4
TOTAL	**225**	**207**	**219**

1/ Excludes estimated accrual payments for civil service retirement and health benefits.

This table shows the budget requests (and for 2002, the actual budget figures) of the Maritime Administration for the years 2003 and 2004, along with a breakdown of how the monies were to be spent. In the past, a major reason for problems in maritime security has been a lack of funding to carry out operations efficiently. As long as Congress continues to appropriate sufficient funds for maritime and port security, the nation will likely enjoy greater safety along its shores and at sea.

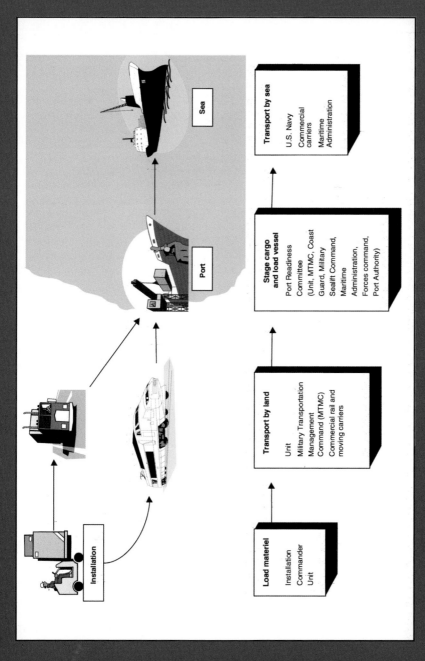

This figure traces the general phases of maritime commerce and outlines which governmental body is responsible for security at each step of the process. Based on data provided by the Department of Defense and published in October 2002, the illustration clearly shows just how in-depth the nation's maritime security has become since the 9/11 attacks.

Maritime security has changed dramatically in the months and years since September 11, 2001. Not only have various agencies linked to maritime been reorganized and better equipped, but there has also been an expanded presence of safety officers all over the nation's coasts. Here, a member of the newly formed Coast Guard Maritime Safety and Security Team (MSST) stands guard near the Brooklyn Bridge. This photograph, taken on September 19, 2002, is a poignant reminder of the heightened state of vigilance in which we now live since the devastating events of 9/11.

whereby the individual executive departments (e.g., transportation, defense, and state) submit their budget requests to the Office of Management and Budget (OMB). The submissions must be received by the OMB by the end of June for analysis. These requests are returned, or "passed back," to the submitting department for "appeal and decision making" and then resubmitted by the end of the following September. After the Office of Management and Budget makes a final review, the president presents his proposed budget to Congress by the first Monday of the following February, at which time it is taken under consideration for action and passage. If all goes well, the process is completed by September, being finalized after Congress returns from summer recess during the latter part of July and early August. When the budget development and approval process runs smoothly, the government has the funds it needs to operate with each fiscal year, beginning October 1.

During the latter 1980s, the 1990s, and the first two years of the twenty-first century, however, the budget approval process was notoriously late as a result of partisan politics and fierce struggles between the White House and Congress over the control of the fiscal process. The two branches of the government argued over the funding of favorite programs, which are often referred to by critics as "pork." When there is no approved budget for the new fiscal year, a system of continuing resolutions is employed: Congress authorizes funding for periods of up to ten days based on the prior year's approved budget; no increases or new programs are allowed. In fiscal year 2001, twenty-one continuing resolutions were needed before the final budget was approved.

PORT SECURITY GRANTS PROGRAM
In the aftermath of September 11, 2001, the strong public reaction to the attacks prompted a security self-analysis that included the maritime industry. Due to the urgency required to shore up and improve security programs, and given the lengthy nature

of the federal budget process, a Port Security Grants program was created by Congress and delivered through the seaport security provisions contained in the Department of Defense Appropriations Act for Fiscal Year 2002. A total of $92.3 million was awarded in 2002 by Secretary of Transportation Norman Y. Mineta to fifty-one ports located throughout the nation. The Transportation Security Administration that managed the program spent five months after the February 2002 broad agency announcement calling for proposals from port and other local authorities and analyzing the requests for funding assistance with advice from the Maritime Administration and the Coast Guard. Working together, these organizations made determinations regarding which ports were most in need of assistance and how much funding they should receive. Most major ports received $2 million to $5 million each to bolster their maritime security programs and infrastructure. The majority of the funding distributed by the Department of Transportation to the ports was used by the various port authorities to perform needed security surveys to analyze maritime threats and vulnerabilities specific to the particular port. The analysis was performed in an effort to mitigate or minimize both potential and real dangers, as determined by the assessments.

As we have discussed, the security assessment or survey is the first step in developing a successful security program. Many of the primary U.S. ports had not been evaluated properly with regard to the type and magnitude of terrorist threat demonstrated on September 11, 2001. In addition, many ports used their Port Security Grant program funding to restore and develop appropriate security infrastructure, including fencing, gates, and detection and identification systems. Most major ports were able to receive enough grant money to perform both the security assessment and the restoration or implementation of the necessary physical or systems security infrastructure. For these ports, bids from commercial security

Funding an Effective Maritime Security Program

The amount of funding required to provide the United States with an effective maritime security program has been and will continue to be a matter of serious debate. Congress and the Bush administration have mandated many new programs designed to improve the security of shipping and ports in the United States but the necessary funding has been slow in coming and few security experts agree that what has been appropriated is adequate for the task at hand. The Transportation Security Administration continues to provide about $120 million per year for the Port Security Grants program, and so far, the major U.S. ports have been able to repair and refurbish their physical infrastructure, including facility perimeter security fencing, threat detection and alarm systems, and automatic identification systems for employees and customers. Additionally, with this grant money, these ports have, for the most part, been able to perform the newly required security assessments and related security plan development processes. The chairman of the House Appropriations Subcommittee on Homeland Security, Representative Harold Rogers (R-KY), reported that within two years after the terrible events of 9/11, "Congress has invested $75.8 billion for homeland security efforts across the federal government and in the homeland security appropriations bill passed by the House on June 24, 2003, the first-ever legislation of its kind, we provide an additional $29.4 billion for the Homeland Security Department in 2004." Chairman Rogers also indicated that the Transportation Security Administration, which had been "provided with more than $10 billion for transportation security efforts," would receive an additional $5 billion proposed for 2004. Rogers added, "Through the Container Security Initiative, we are moving our zone of security outward and are continuing to inspect 100 percent of all high-interest cargo and vessels coming into our waters." With regard to a best cost-analysis approach, Rogers recommended that the government take "a hard look at our vulnerabilities and apply funding accordingly." This was good advice from a seasoned and expert appropriator.

Some security experts argue that maritime does not receive its fair share of the homeland-security budget, but if the terrorist threat, based on the best intelligence available, continues to focus on the aviation industry, then the slow but steady pace of the Port Security Grants program may be a realistic and reliable approach to shore up the vulnerabilities of U.S. ports. However, the Container Security Initiative program will continue to be fatally flawed until total global coverage is achieved. Having U.S. Customs agents at the top twenty container ports in the world is nowhere near the ideal "trusted agent" presence desired at all container ports from which potential weapons of mass destruction could originate.

concerns were solicited and contracts were awarded so that the necessary work could be performed as dictated by the findings of the security assessment.

A typical example of this process would be the award by the Port of Oakland (which calls itself "the nation's fourth busiest container port") of a $4.75 million maritime security enhancement contract to Florida-based ADT Security Services, Inc., for the design and installation of an integrated security system. The contract calls for a comprehensive system that uses the most advanced security technology available, including automated access control, video surveillance, and perimeter intrusion detection devices integrated in an innovative wireless communications and alarm system. The use of wireless and encrypted technology allows the elimination of over 31 miles (50 kilometers) of electrical trenching that permits the uninterrupted operation of the terminals within the port and saves millions of dollars in labor and construction expense. Based on the contract, ten terminals within the Port of Oakland Authority would be outfitted with the new technology, so that terminal operators can be provided with firewalled, password-protected command and control systems using a Web-enabled remote management program. Once installed, the new program's hardware and software would enable port security authorities to share video and data with local, state, and federal enforcement agencies that exercise police jurisdiction over the port. The enforcement agencies will include the U.S. Coast Guard, the Transportation and Security Administration, the Bureau of Customs and Border Protection, the California Highway Patrol, the Alameda County Sheriffs Department, and the Oakland Police Department. With this state-of-the-art program, the Port of Oakland will be able to meet the new federal Homeland Security Department requirements as delineated in the Maritime Transportation Security Act. It will also continue to operate with efficiently moving cargo throughput.

Without the federally initiated Port Security Grants program, the Port of Oakland and most others would have been unable to move forward so quickly with their security improvement programs. Because most major ports have developed in step with economic cycles and transitions, they have become a varied series of separately located terminals delivering passengers and freight, including wet and dry bulk and container traffic. Each terminal requires a unique security program based on size, location, and geographic characteristics, among other variables. Only a massive and immediate federal spending program could provide the means to achieve the scale and effectiveness that a comprehensive and expensive security system delivers.

For smaller ports and individual terminals (which may or may not be part of a huge port complex like the Oakland Port Authority), even the costs for the most basic perimeter security hardware may be beyond their fundraising or capital development capabilities. For the most part, federal awards were granted to these facilities also in the period after 9/11. For instance, the required terminal facility fencing (eight-foot-high cyclone wire with an additional foot of three-strand barbed or concertina wire angled outward at forty-five degrees) costs fifteen dollars per foot. Required terminal access gates and associated fittings are twelve dollars per square foot. Effective state-of-the-art closed-circuit television, and laser beam and motion detection systems for a typical 100-by-200-yard terminal area cost approximately $100,000. Systems for credentialing and identifying transportation workers can cost upward of $30,000 for an operation that employs twenty-five or fewer people. And this estimate includes only equipment used in the daily entry and exit procedure—not the background investigation process.

Although the cost of an effective port security program in most cases is huge, only a part of the necessary funding has been provided by federal grants. The question of how to pay for the appropriate level of safety and security for U.S ports was discussed in Congress during the debates on the passage of the Maritime Transportation Security Act in 2002. The initially proposed legislation called for a harbor use tax that would have generated revenue based on the tonnage of any particular shipment of cargo passing through a port or terminal facility. After analysis, discussion, and debate by both the Senate and House of Representative transportation committees, in the end, it was decided that no new taxes would be created as part of an effort to support the slowly recovering domestic and global economy.

FUNDING PHASE TWO

In order to continue the development of the port security momentum established by the Port Security Grants program of 2002, Secretary Mineta announced in early 2003 a "phase two" that would supply an additional $104 million to critical national seaports to finance the cost of enhancing facility and operational security. Applications in support of seaport security would be accepted for two major categories. The first was a continuation of the original phase one, offered the previous year. This category included port or terminal security assessments that would ascertain vulnerabilities and identify mitigation strategies, which would serve to finalize the port security survey process. The second category was intended to enhance port facility and operational security through the design and implementation of facility access control, physical security, and cargo and passenger security. Also included in the second phase was an additional $28 million to fund Operation Safe Cargo, a pilot program partnering the U.S. Bureau of Customs and Border Patrol with port authorities and other law enforcement agencies in an effort to promote cargo container security.

Once again, the Bush administration and Congress had found a way to keep funding available for the ports. Phase two was to be administered again by the Transportation Security Administration with the assistance of the U.S. Coast Guard and the Maritime Administration. Despite these major steps forward, substantially more funding should and must be budgeted, appropriated, and spent annually by the federal government in order to continue the development and maintenance of an effective U.S. port security program. With two large moves in the right direction made possible thanks to the Port Security Grants program, U.S. ports have a foothold, if not a foundation, to build upon.

6

Long-term
Maritime Security

The immediate steps taken by the United States in reaction to events of 9/11 were swift and effective. In addition to these steps, a longer-term program was being developed, sometimes in fits and starts, but always moving forward toward an effective yet efficient system of national maritime security.

THE MARITIME TRANSPORTATION SECURITY ACT

The Maritime Transportation Security Act signed into law by President George W. Bush in November 2002 laid the groundwork for a comprehensive package of maritime and port security legislation that will be applied over a period of at least five years. Development and passage of the Maritime Transportation Security Act was the result of the work of the Senate Committee on Commerce, Science, and Transportation, chaired by Senator Fritz Hollings (D-SC) and the House Committee on Infrastructure and Transportation, chaired by Representative Don Young (R-AK). Based on the findings of the Clinton Port Security Commission and the testimony of many maritime security experts from the government, the transportation and security industries, and academia, many new concepts have been integrated into traditional security practices. Many of these new ideas have been made possible by significant advancements in technology.

The Clinton Port Security Commission provided the self-review and analysis necessary to begin the fundamental government interagency reorganization, both federal and local. The commission also created a fairly current security assessment for many major U.S. ports.

The Maritime Transportation Security Act defines the tremendous scope of U.S. port security challenges by citing the huge numbers of ports, personnel, cargos, and vessels affected by security threats. All these factors come into play when developing threat mitigation and vulnerability solutions. The act declares that 361 domestic ports are critical to over 95 percent of U.S. overseas trade, which includes bulk cargo, containerized cargo, and passengers. The number also includes ferries that transport 113 million passengers and 32,000 vehicles per year. The threats defined in the act include large-scale terrorist attacks that might cause considerable loss of life or economic disruption, drug trafficking, cargo theft, and smuggling of contraband and aliens. The act emphasizes that it is in the best interests of the U.S. economy to encourage the free flow of interstate and foreign commerce, as well as safe and efficient movement of cargo. The act acknowledges the special risks to passenger vessels and weaknesses in cargo tracking and verification. It proposes to implement new instruments that will enhance an improved global security system. The act credits the work of the Interagency Commission on Crime and Security in the United States Ports (the Clinton Port Security Commission) and also the efforts of the International Maritime Organization in helping to create and implement the new global security system. Furthermore, the act requires the secretary of transportation (or, more specifically, the secretary of the department in which the Coast Guard is operating) to conduct and oversee a variety of measures to improve the safety at ports and on vessels. These safety measures are widened to include a more intensive spectrum of maritime threats.

The Maritime Transportation Security Act focuses on facility and vessel vulnerability and security assessments. According to the act, the secretary or the facility or vessel's owner or operator may conduct the assessment if the secretary deems that the issues mentioned by the act are adequately addressed. Assessments are to be updated every five years at a minimum.

THE NATIONAL MARITIME TRANSPORTATION SECURITY PLAN

The act further stipulates that the secretary establish a National Maritime Transportation Security Plan. Here again, in the security world, security assessments lead logically to security plans. The plan should be comprehensive in nature in order to deter and respond to a transportation security incident, which, per the act, is the new terminology for a terrorist attack on the transportation system. The plan must provide for the assignment of duties and responsibilities among identified federal, state, and local security departments and agencies. The plan calls for the creation of a system of surveillance and notification to forecast imminent threats of transportation security incidents, the establishment of a risk-based system for evaluating the potential for violations of security areas, and the designation of areas where Area Maritime Transportation Security Plans apply.

Plans will be implemented by a Coast Guard official, who will be the Federal Maritime Security Coordinator for a specific area and utilize Coast Guard maritime teams to maintain safety and security. The Area Security Advisory Committee—composed of security-related experts from government, industry, and academia appointed by the secretary—will advise the Area Maritime Security Coordinator. The coordinators will develop individual Area Maritime Security Plans and integrate their own plans with those of other areas as part of the national plan. They will also synchronize operations with the Department of Defense with regard to Defense-controlled facilities, vessels, and equipment. All area plans must be updated at least every five years. Vessel and facility security plans are submitted to the secretary by the vessel and facility operators within six months after the issue of interim final regulations on vessel and facility security plans. Any vessel or facility for which a security plan is required may not operate after the twelve-month period following the prescription of the interim final regulations on vessel and facility security plans. Exceptions are made for vessels or facilities that have plans that are approved or waived by the secretary.

An additional requirement of the act calls for the issuance of biometric transportation security cards to workers who must be admitted to secure transportation areas. These areas are specified in security plans if the secretary determines that they pose no risk to security. The act directs the attorney general, upon the request of the secretary, to perform background records checks requiring security risk analysis. Both of these procedures are meant to assist the transportation industry in eliminating any criminal or high-risk persons within the ranks of the employed.

Further requirements call for the establishment of a foreign port and foreign-flagged vessel analysis program. In this program, foreign ports and foreign-flagged vessels that fail to meet the newly established global security standards will be singled out and monitored until they comply with the new security programs. Automatic identification system (AIS) requirements are emphasized for vessels sailing in U.S. waters if their length is greater than 65 feet or if they are classified as a passenger vessel.

In addition to the vessel tracking requirements inherent in the AIS policy, Customs Service reporting by carriers and shippers for transshipped (reassigned to another carrier) and idle cargo and containers is refined and delineated with specific time limits. This minimizes the risk of illegal shipments and cargo tampering. The act also provides for various funding mechanisms, including a system of reporting and oversight that makes sure all deadlines, requirements, and financial measures are met in strict accordance with the law. The Port Security Grants program is included as part of the funding mechanism as well.

THE ISPS CODE

While the Maritime Transportation Security Act of 2002 establishes a comprehensive and far-reaching maritime security program specifically for the United States, the International Maritime

Organization (IMO; based in London) has developed a global maritime security program that was driven by U.S. Coast Guard recommendations and proposals. The Coast Guard made these recommendations in November 2001, soon after the tragic events of 9/11. This program, called the International Code for the Security of Ships and of Port Facilities (or ISPS Code), was approved by the IMO in December 2002. It is generally consistent and was developed in parallel with the Maritime Transportation Security Act.

The objectives of the ISPS Code are global and apply to the

Clay Tiles and the Container Security Initiative

The MV *Palermo Senator*, a Liberian-flagged container ship bound for Elizabeth, New Jersey, and the Port of Newark was searched off the coast of New Jersey based on intelligence suggesting that it might be carrying weapons of mass destruction into the United States. Initial readings taken on board the vessel indicated levels of both neutron and gamma emissions, which became cause for concern. The fact that President Bush was nearby in New York City for ceremonies commemorating the one-year anniversary of 9/11 made the situation even more serious. The ship was detained at sea, miles away from the coastline, while teams of security experts and government scientists pored over its cargo to determine the magnitude of the potential threat. Special Operations forces and the Energy Department's Nuclear Energy Search Team (NEST) spent three days searching the cargo containers on board the *Palermo Senator*, which had sailed from Valencia, Spain, but had previously made stops in Bandar Abbas, Iran; Jeddah, Saudi Arabia; and Karachi, Pakistan. The NEST mission is to detect, dismantle, and dispose of weapons of mass destruction, and NEST squads have been used since their establishment in 1974 to investigate and analyze suspicious radiological devices. After a detailed search and analysis, it was determined by the on-scene investigators that the source of radioactivity was a container full of ordinary clay tiles. Small amounts of radioactive emission, referred to as background radiation, is common in many natural materials that are shipped regularly as containerized cargo and the *Palermo Senator* incident served to emphasize the dilemmas involved in the search for weapons of mass destruction within the global transportation system. Searching a ship at sea is a difficult process, because containers are tightly spaced and stacked on top of one another. If seas are rough, the task may become impossible for safety's sake. The example of the *Palermo Senator* also points out the effectiveness of the Customs Service Automated Targeting System and the need to inspect high-interest cargo at its port of origin, both fundamental processes in the Customs Bureau's Container Security Initiative.

contracting governments. These governments include more than 120 signatory countries and all of the leading maritime nations. The requirements of the ISPS Code include maritime security intelligence gathering and assessment, maritime security communications, prevention of unauthorized access to ships and ports and their restricted areas, and prevention of the introduction of unauthorized weapons or explosives to ships or port facilities. Also included are the provision of alarms to issue an alert to security threats and incidents, the development of ship and port facility security plans based upon related security assessments, and the training, drills, and exercises needed to provide proficiency in regard to all the other requirements. A three-tiered system of minimum protective security, additional protective security based on heightened risk, and further specific security based on probable or imminent security incidents is emphasized.

The ISPS Code is compulsory for cargo vessels of 500 gross tons or greater, all passenger vessels, and mobile offshore drilling units. Port facilities serving such vessels engaged on international voyages are also subject to the code. Contracting governments' duties are defined in the code and their rights to delegate certain of these to responsible security organizations (RSOs) are discussed as well.

DECLARATION OF SECURITY

The Declaration of Security is a document used to assess interface between ship and port. It can be originated by both ships and port facilities to determine or verify credible security programs. The document must be completed by the appropriate parties in charge of the involved ships and ports. Shipping company security responsibilities and ship requirements are defined for all three security levels. They include controlling access to the ship, controlling the embarkation of persons and their effects, monitoring restricted areas to ensure that only authorized personnel gain admittance, monitoring deck areas and areas surrounding the ship, supervising the handling of cargo and ships' stores, and ensuring that security communications are adequate and available.

The ship security assessment and its relationship to the ship security plan are delineated in accordance with the preceding shipping company responsibilities, as are the port facility assessment and plan requirements. The port facility security responsibilities include controlling access to the port facility, monitoring of the facility (including anchoring and berthing areas), monitoring restricted areas to ensure that only the authorized have access, supervising the handling of cargo and ships' stores, and keeping security communications and alarms ready and available. The code emphasizes that, although any of the recognized security organizations may develop security assessments and plans, only contracting governments may actually approve them.

The Declaration of Security Document details the duties of the Ship Security Officer, the Company Security Officer, and the Port Facility Security Officer. The document lists both ship and port facility security qualifications and elaborates on appropriate training, drills, and exercises, including the type and frequency. It also details storage and maintenance procedures.

The code emphasizes that security measures and procedures shall be applied at the port facility in such a manner as to cause a minimum of interference with, or delay to, passengers, ships, ships' personnel and visitors, and goods and services. Verification and certification for ship security requirements are outlined in the code and a sample International Ship Security Certificate is attached for inspection. The certificate issuance and endorsement process, as well as duration and validity, are explained. In general, there is no more than five years between certificate renewals.

Part A of the code lists all mandatory requirements for ships and port facilities, while the more detailed Part B provides general guidance for the implementation of the regulations laid out in Part A. Most security experts believe that the code will be adopted by the IMO as it evolves and as time permits. The IMO accepts the process of training and qualification to enhance the capabilities of ship and port facility security programs. Part B of the code also includes a sample Declaration of Security document with endorsement for verifications. It encourages the promotion of mutual technical assistance between contracting governments, advocates the enhancement of security in cooperation with the International Labor Organization and seafarers' and transportation workers' identity cards, and promotes the cooperation of the World Customs Organization. The World Customs Organization addresses the improved security of closed cargo container units, including the use of long- and short-range ship and cargo identification and tracking systems.

MARITIME SECURITY GUIDELINES

To support the implementation of both the Maritime Transportation Security Act and the International Ship and Port Facility Security Code, the U.S. Coast Guard has issued three Navigation and Vessel Inspection Circulars that contain security guidelines for cargo vessels, passenger vessels, and port facilities. These circulars present risk-based management and analysis techniques to develop mitigation and countermeasure strategies to defeat any perceived maritime security threat.

The U.S. Bureau of Customs and Border Patrol, in a similar supportive program, has developed the Custom-Trade Partnership against Terrorism (C-TPAT). This program requires all participating members to comply entirely with the latest security regulations or risk increased scrutiny of cargo and documentation. Such scrutiny may create trade and commerce disadvantages for offenders or for those that do not qualify. The Maritime Transportation Security Act, the International Ship and Port Facility Security Code, the new U.S. Coast Guard Security Navigation and Vessel Inspection Circulars, and the U.S. Bureau of Customs and Border Protection Custom-Trade Partnership against Terrorism are critical security programs, all of which have been created since, and as a result of, the catastrophic events of 9/11. With luck, their effectiveness will be proven and expanded upon with the passage of time.

7

Awareness, Vigilance, Training, and Homeland Security

Since the tragic events of September 11, 2001, the United States has developed many initiatives to overcome the perceived weaknesses in the U.S. homeland-security program. The government has sponsored efforts for terrorist threat and vulnerability analysis. In addition, a movement began in Congress to establish a new, separate government department that would pull together the many diverse security functions. These security duties were scattered far and wide across the federal bureaucracy. A new department would be dedicated to the unification of all efforts to establish a better awareness of the global threat of terrorism for both government and citizens. This department would also be dedicated to setting up an improved security infrastructure, including the policies, procedures, and training needed to successfully maintain a renewed vigilance. Security efforts would be focused on defeating the threat of terrorism while guaranteeing the type of safe and efficient transportation system that is critical to the advancement of global freedom and prosperity.

THE HOMELAND SECURITY DEPARTMENT

The Bush administration's plans for improving homeland security had been initiated as early as May 2001, when President George W. Bush directed Vice President Dick Cheney to take charge of establishing a counterterrorism system that would protect the United States from weapons of mass destruction. Despite this early effort, the Bush administration initially opposed the immediate clamor to reorganize government security programs after 9/11. In June 2002, however, the administration unexpectedly announced a plan for the new Homeland Security Department. Under this plan, most of the diverse and widespread security-related agencies, bureaus, and offices in the federal government would become part of an entirely new executive branch department. Analysis of national security performed by a congressional-appointed commission headed by former Senators Warren Rudman (R-NH) and Gary Hart (D-CO) as early as the spring of 2000 had recommended the formation of a Homeland Security Department. However, their recommendation envisioned a much smaller department than the one proposed by the Bush administration.

Bush appointed Governor Tom Ridge of Pennsylvania to head the new department (which actually began in 2001 as the non-cabinet Office of Homeland Security). Although Ridge was officially the administration's key representative for home-land-security issues, he had neither sufficient funding nor decision-making authority in the vast government security bureaucracy. The Bush administration's move to reestablish its leadership in the war against terrorism in Afghanistan by urging the Congress to create a Homeland Security Department in a nationwide presidential television broadcast on the evening of June 6, 2002, took many by surprise. The planned details for the new department had been worked out privately among a few top-level administration staff members in the months preceding the broadcast.

THE VISION FOR HOMELAND SECURITY
The Bush administration's vision for the new Homeland Security Department included large amounts of the executive branch that had previously been dedicated to the security of the United States and its borders. The department would

also engage in the day-to-day administration and oversight of normal trade, commerce, and safety against natural and accidental disasters. The Coast Guard, Secret Service, Federal Emergency Management Agency, Customs Service, Border Patrol, Immigration and Naturalization Service, and the newly created Transportation and Security Administration were to be combined to form a brand-new department—an organization exceeded in size only by the Veterans Administration and the Department of Defense.

The mission of the new department would be to coordinate intelligence regarding terrorism and improve the nation's security perimeter and domestic defenses. In his live White House address to Congress and the people of the United States, President George W. Bush stated, "As we have learned more about the plans and capabilities of the terrorist network, we have concluded that our government must be reorganized to deal more effectively with the new threats of the 21st century." Bush went on to say that nothing he was aware of could have prevented the horror of September 11, 2001. However, based on the knowledge acquired by the intelligence and security community since then, it was clear that errors had been made in regard to security that might possibly have stopped the attacks. Now, however, there was no alternative but to move forward with a powerful and comprehensive home-land-security program like the one embodied in the new Homeland Security Department.

Missing from the recommended departmental elements were both the Federal Bureau of Investigation (FBI) and the Central Intelligence Agency (CIA), each of which had come under recent scrutiny and criticism by Congress and the media. Both had been exposed for bureaucratic infighting as a result of the scrutiny of their methods after 9/11. The new Homeland Security Department formation would affect more than 170,000 existing government jobs and would demand an annual budget of between $30 billion and $40 billion.

One of the new Homeland Security Department's key missions was to close the gaps that had existed between the previously separate security organizations. All of the older agencies had their own cultures and bureaucratic dynamics, which, in practice, worked against the success of the overall domestic U.S. security program. Many people have felt that the weaknesses and vulnerabilities discovered in the government's security policies and procedures (with respect to the newly defined global terrorism threat) would be better mitigated by a more effectively organized, coordinated, and focused Homeland Security Department.

MEMBERS OF THE HOMELAND SECURITY DEPARTMENT

There was a significant period of analysis and debate among the Bush administration, the Senate, the House of Representatives, and security experts from all areas, including government, industry, and academia, during the summer and fall of 2002. The original White House proposal for the new department called for the organization to be formed and in operation by January 2003. It envisioned the new Homeland Security Department being composed of four directorates. The first directorate would manage border transportation and security, and would consist of the Immigration and Naturalization Service (from the Justice Department), the Customs Service (from the Treasury Department), the Coast Guard (from the Department of Transportation), the Animal and Plant Health Protection Inspection Service (from the Agriculture Department), the Federal Protective Service (from the General Services Administration), and the Transportation Security Administration (from the Transportation Department). A second directorate, concerned with emergency preparedness and response, would include the Federal Emergency Management Agency (FEMA, an independent government agency); chemical, biological, radiological, and nuclear response assets (from the Health and Human Services Department); the Domestic Emergency

Support Team (from the Justice Department); the Nuclear Incident Response Team (from the Department of Energy); the National Domestic Preparedness Office (from the FBI); and the Federal Law Enforcement Training Center (from the Treasury Department). The third directorate would be in charge of chemical, biological, radiological, and nuclear counter-measures. It would include the Lawrence Livermore National Laboratory, the Civilian Bio-defense Research Program (from the Health and Human Services Department), and the Plum Island Animal Disease Center (from the Agriculture Department). The fourth and final directorate—dedicated to information analysis and infrastructure protection—was to be composed of the Critical Infrastructure Assurance Office (from the Commerce Department), the Federal Computer Incident Response Center (from the General Services Administration), the National Communications Systems (from the Department of Defense), the National Infrastructure Protection Center (from the FBI), and the National Infrastructure Simulation and Analysis Center (from the Energy Department).

The Secret Service (from the Treasury Department) would remain a separate entity, reporting directly to the secretary of the Homeland Security Department. The Secret Service would specialize in threat assessments while also continuing to protect the president and other key governmental leaders. The FBI and CIA would also be kept separate and would provide police operations and forensics investigation, and intelligence, respec-tively, as required.

This massive and complex organizational structure was designed to correct the weaknesses and mitigate the vulnerabilities that had been identified during the comprehensive government and private analysis that took place during the first year after the 9/11 terrorist attacks. Certain weaknesses and vulnerabilities were deemed to be pervasive across the U.S. transportation network, which included aviation, rail, trucking, and pipelines, in addition to maritime facilities and vessels.

Assigning the Blame

Where were antiterrorist awareness, training, and vigilance levels before September 11, 2001? Many security experts and government officials have been busy analyzing that question and many U.S. citizens and loved ones and friends of the victims are very interested in their findings. The Congressional Joint Committee on Intelligence released a report on July 24, 2003, condemning the U.S. intelligence community for errors and investigative missteps that, if avoided, might have prevented the horrible events of 9/11 from happening. Other agencies of the government, including the Immigration and Naturalization Service and the Federal Aviation Administration (FAA), as part of the new Homeland Security Department are in the process of correcting flawed procedures that contributed to the ease with which the terrorists were able to accomplish their grisly deeds. The FBI had information as far back as 1998 indicating that Osama bin Laden's associates were planning to hijack planes and had successfully discovered methods of evading security at a New York airport. The CIA's lack of interest in Osama bin Laden prevented the U.S. military from being able to target him once his Afghan camps had been discovered. Many pieces of useful evidence at both the FBI and CIA had been filed prematurely and had not found its way to the appropriate officials. The INS, on the other hand, had allowed a massive number of illegal aliens—including the hijackers—to remain in the United States under foreign student status without satisfying the required reporting procedures. Congress was guilty of underfunding the INS and of providing insufficient support in the implementation and application of immigration laws based on the special business interests of their constituents. The Patriot Act and the reassignment of INS to the Homeland Security Department have improved this situation, but many loopholes remain for illegal aliens. The FAA sky marshal program was undermanned and, at the time of 9/11, it had fewer than fifty marshals assigned. The growth of the sky marshal program to include between 4,000 and 5,000 personnel and its transferal to the Transportation Security Administration has improved its ability to provide security in the air. Although 9/11 was primarily an aviation event, it is easy to compare the pre-9/11 shortcomings and errors in the aviation industry to those that existed in maritime. There were not—and still aren't—enough Coast Guard assets, either personnel or equipment, to patrol all the nation's coasts and harbors. There was no system for tracking and identifying all high-interest vessels entering and leaving U.S. ports. And finally, the Coast Guard's Captains of the Port did not have sufficient authority, direction, or personnel to effectively enforce the oversight of vessel and port security programs. The passage of the Maritime Transportation Security Act is an attempt to correct these inadequacies. Only time will tell how successful it will be.

MARITIME SECURITY CONCERNS

The two major areas of security concern within the maritime sector involve the detection of terrorists and their weapons of mass destruction and the protection of U.S. ports, facilities, and ships from these threats. The fear is that weapons of mass destruction may be concealed in containerized cargo. An immediate and continued solution for cargo container security and inspection has been the increased use of X-ray detection devices on high-risk containers. Containers of high interest are flagged by a centralized Customs Service cargo tracking and analysis database. Agreements with foreign governments to allow U.S. Customs inspection of inbound U.S. cargo at foreign port locations is part of the Cargo Security Initiative program. These inspections have expanded to include the top forty world ports, a difficult diplomatic and day-to-day transportation operation. Because of the enormous volume of incoming containers, it is difficult to inspect all the containers, and only about 2 percent of the 6 million containers that come in each year are inspected at U.S. ports. That means the Cargo Security Initiative applies to only about half of the world's maritime container trade.

The safety and security of U.S. ports has improved greatly as a result of an increase in Coast Guard patrols, boarding equipment, and personnel; greater support from state and local law enforcement assets; and a 96-hour notice of port arrival requirement for vessels. However, funding cutbacks and the more than 11,000 miles (17,706 kilometers) of coastline make a zero-defect coastal security program impossible. The Bush administration nevertheless has asserted that steady maritime security progress has been made in the war against terrorism. In the administration's view, a proposal for the development of an official Homeland Security Department was the next critical step in continuing this progress. However, the House and Senate analysis of the Bush administration proposal was made especially complicated by the fact that more than 88 congressional committees would be impacted by the changes called for in the new proposal, because of the consolidation of 22 former agencies.

THE HOMELAND SECURITY DEPARTMENT BECOMES OFFICIAL

Still, few members of Congress dared to oppose the formation of the new department, because the events and aftermath of 9/11 had galvanized the American consciousness into a dedicated and deliberate instrument to be used to defeat the development and spread of global terrorism. Many lawmakers, while applauding the formation of the new organization, took issue with its size and its control over existing agencies—particularly medical and health safety organizations that were already performing effectively.

In July 2002, the Bush administration added an additional proposal that included a sweeping homeland-security strategy to be implemented by the Homeland Security Department. The idea advocated the employment of "red team" practices, so that weaknesses could be discovered in the nation's critical infrastructure. It also included the expansion of extradition practices and standardization of travel documents with other countries in order to limit terrorist movement, the creation of terrorism insurance for business and property owners, the revision of secrecy laws to prevent general public knowledge of vulnerabilities, the enhancement of federal, state, and local government cooperation, and computer security. Lastly, the strategy included the addition of new vessels and equipment to the Coast Guard antiterror mission and an increased emphasis on the monitoring of the 16 million shipping containers that enter or cross the United States annually.

After much interaction between the Bush administration and Congress on the nature and details of the new

Homeland Security Department, consensus was finally reached in November 2002. The House version of the Homeland Security Act was passed on November 13, 2002. It called for the "protection of America, its seaports, nuclear plants, energy pipelines and other infrastructure" by gathering and disseminating intelligence information to well-trained "police officers, firefighters and health workers" armed with new technology and threat detection devices. The Senate version of the Homeland Security Act was passed on November 19, 2002. President George W. Bush signed the Homeland Security Act into law on November 24, 2002, nominating Tom Ridge as its secretary.

SPEEDY RESPONSE TO ATTACKS

The Bush administration had pushed hard for the relatively quick legislative approval. It had overcome criticism from senior members of Congress on workers' rights with regard to national security, as well as the necessity to include so many agencies for the success of the department. The Bush administration had busily engaged in the war against terrorism and had an impressive record of accomplishments to show for its efforts, most of which culminated in the formation of the Homeland Security Department. It was not a coincidence that President George W. Bush signed the Maritime Transportation Security Act on the same day he signed the Homeland Security Department legislation, and a day later, approved legislation for terrorism insurance.

With the establishment of the Homeland Security Department, there would be enhanced and heightened security awareness through greater coordination, better-defined operational responsibilities, and technological advances among members of both the security and intelligence communities. There was also provision for increased vigilance through the unification of all the appropriate security agencies in the government. In addition, a critical emphasis was placed on the maintenance and intensity of their programs through effective, unified, and continuously occurring training programs directed by the Homeland Security Department. The most critical requirement for a successful U.S. homeland-security plan—the unification of government agencies with powerful leadership had been put into place.

8

The Way Forward in the New World

Since September 11, 2001, the U.S. maritime security program has come a long way. The self-analysis stemming from the terrorist attacks has been both profound and unnerving. As a result, the appropriate discourse and planning have taken place to prevent future attacks from striking maritime targets. Of course, plans are still being implemented according to priorities, and plans are changing due to intelligence analysis, funding, and the sometimes excruciatingly slow pace of the political process. Despite these delays, the federal government has led the in-depth maritime security evaluation process with remarkable speed.

Some state governments, most notably Florida, have made impressive advances in maritime security. Florida maritime security statutes, which require comprehensive port and terminal facility security programs (beginning with the security survey and assessment process) were passed in January 2001, well in advance of the wake-up call delivered at the World Trade Center and the Pentagon the following September. Other major coastal states that maintain substantial port and intermodal transportation facilities may soon be enacting maritime security legislation similar to that of Florida to strengthen the security of our nation's ports and coastlines.

THE SLEEPING GIANT

Compared to other modes of transportation, including aviation, trucking, and rail, the maritime industry appears to be at great risk for terrorist attacks. This perception is due to the built-in vulnerability that results from our free and open society and system of trade, our seemingly limitless and difficult-to-patrol coastline, and the inherent lack of security and process control that has become institutionalized over time in the global transportation system. However, maritime is no different from other modes of transportation. For example, similar vulnerabilities existed in aviation prior to the tragic events of September 11, 2001.

Awareness of terrorist sects has existed since the late 1980s. This intelligence is based on public comments made by well-known and influential government figures, such as Lieutenant Colonel Oliver North. At the time of the Iran-Contra Scandal in 1987, North publicly described the operations of Osama bin Laden and the Al Qaeda network in the Middle East. This is noteworthy due to the apparent failure of the appropriate government organizations to investigate and give effective notice to the executive and legislative branches that might have attempted to prevent terrorist-sponsored events such as those of September 11, 2001. This inaction becomes very disturbing when viewed against the terrorist events involving the initial truck bombing of the World Trade Center in 1993 and its storied aftermath—including the trial and conviction of the terrorists, the bombing of the U.S. embassies in Nairobi and Dar Es Salaam, and the bombing of the U.S.S. *Cole* in Aden only a year before the events of September 11, 2001.

FILLING INTELLIGENCE GAPS

The recent analysis of the FBI and CIA's difficulties to coordinate and process intelligence vital to the security of the United States has been the subject of much interest to the many congressional and government-appointed "blue ribbon" panels investigating the events of September 11, 2001. Organizational mission and design problems and bureaucratic politics and infighting should not result in an event as tragic as that of September 11, 2001, but there are many defenders of both the CIA and FBI. These defenders, including Attorney General John Ashcroft, feel that the crime-fighting and intelligence-gathering capabilities of these two organizations have been extremely curtailed or limited. They believe much needs to be done on a permanent basis so the FBI and CIA can perform their jobs more effectively and provide the proper level of safety and security for U.S. citizens.

Add to these intelligence challenges the problem of the huge number of Middle Eastern illegal aliens the Immigration and Naturalization Service has been attempting to monitor and control over the years. These illegal aliens have been allowed to roam the United States using expired documents. They have apparently slipped outside the monitoring controls and requirements that were established by law but have been diluted by inconsistent day-to-day INS policy and procedure, which is unduly influenced by international politics and the U.S. economy.

Finally, but not least importantly, there was the Federal Aviation Administration (FAA) practice of concentrating its sky marshal assets primarily on international, rather than domestic, flights. This vulnerability in the security of the U.S. domestic aviation sector was exacerbated by the small total number of sky marshals authorized for use in the FAA security program.

When viewed against the steps taken by the U.S. government, led by the Bush administration and Congress since September 11, 2001, many of the vulnerabilities in intelligence gathering and security agency coordination and operation have been legislatively mitigated by the Aviation and Transportation Security Act, the Maritime Transportation and Security Act, and the legislation forming the Homeland Security Department. Combined with the promise of ostensibly capable and motivated leadership to responsibly oversee the day-to-day management of this very comprehensive and far-reaching transportation security program, the general level of safety and awareness in the transportation sector has never been higher.

Additionally, the Patriot Act, signed into law on October 26, 2002, brought greater tracking and interrogation capabilities to law enforcement personnel. These capabilities have been employed in pursuit of illegal aliens and have also provided rules preventing the laundering of terrorist-related funding. The Trade Act of 2002 (signed on July 1, 2002) required the electronic transmission of cargo manifest information to the Customs Service twenty-four hours before the cargo was to be shipped from any port of origin. Together, these acts continue the mitigation of the vulnerability to the terrorist threats present in the United States.

FORMAL THREAT-RISK ANALYSIS

Although the maritime industry didn't feel the shock of the terrorist thunderbolt of September 11, 2001, directly, it was nonetheless forced to evaluate its risks and vulnerabilities in what had become a dramatically different world. Just as aviation had been used for terrorist purposes on 9/11, the maritime industry might well be the vehicle used to perpetrate the next terrorist attack.

An examination of the maritime mode of transportation must include an analysis of its linkages with the rail and trucking industries (in both process and documentation) due to the evolution of today's intermodal systems and their close relationship with one another. An examination of risk in maritime transportation can be made using the popular risk assessment process. This process equates the level of risk in any situation with its worth, or criticality, factored with the known threat and its assessed vulnerabilities. That is, Risk equals Worth times Threat times Vulnerability. First used by Gale Hawkes in his IMO-sponsored port security seminars (held during 2002 at several of the world's busiest container ports), this method of analysis is widely accepted by security experts. It gives a dynamic and accurate assessment of the various scenarios in the U.S. maritime security spectrum. Worst-case maritime scenarios that require this assessment would include at least one of the following: a liquid natural gas refinery or vessel explosion, a weapon of mass destruction detonation at a container terminal or on a vessel in port, the hijacking and destruction of a cruise vessel or ferry, or the use of any of the aforementioned vessels as collision weapons.

The Maritime Threat

Is there a real maritime threat out there or is it just a perceived one and part of the paranoia associated with the aftermath of 9/11? Many security experts and government officials are concerned about the magnitude and probability of the threat to ships and ports because the vulnerabilities are certainly evident. The potential problems have been defined and are being worked on, some faster than others. If a target is not viewed as critical or if terrorists do not wish to attack the target because of its complexity or their lack of expertise with it, then even an apparently severe vulnerability is greatly diminished. Counterterrorist experts tell us that terrorists tend to continue doing what they have been successful at in the past. Typically, that means kidnapping, hijacking, and explosive detonations are—and will continue to be—their weapons of choice. In the maritime scenario, this knowledge would lead us to focus on cruise-liner hijackings and explosive devices that might be hidden within cargo shipments. Cruise-liner security requirements and technology are up and in place, and so are awareness, training, and vigilance. As a result, we may have successfully mitigated the terrorist threat in that arena. For bulk cargo vessels and related terminals, when hazardous materials are involved, the risk is higher because the value of the target and the catastrophe that might result from an attack are larger. For container vessels and terminals, the risk is high because of the inherent inability to eliminate the threat of a hidden device, since close examination of every container would result in a paralysis of commerce. In the July 1, 2003, Federal Register, the U.S. Coast Guard published a list of maritime scenarios with their related risk magnitudes based on the report of many security experts, risk consultants, and government officials who had performed a rigorous analysis using a method called the National Risk Assessment Tool (N-RAT). This technique incorporated the concepts of threat, vulnerability, and consequence in determining risk. Ferries on international voyages were rated with the highest relative risk, largely due to their high-value cargo and the ease with which they may be attacked. Other aspects of maritime commerce, including containerized shipping and offshore chemical facilities, were also included in the higher risk group. Department of Homeland Security Secretary Tom Ridge, in an interview on national television on August 1, 2003, insisted that steps are being taken to move America's security perimeter outward so that its ports will serve as "the last line of defense." Ridge went on to declare that public and government vigilance is "heightened" and will maintain the progress that has been made against terrorism by the Bush administration. As renowned security expert Gale Hawkes advises in his primer, *Maritime Security*, first published in 1989, those who "persist in refusing to consider maritime security seriously may well live to regret their struthious [ostrich-like] attitude."

THREAT-RISK SCENARIOS

To assess the scenario of the liquefied natural gas vessel explosion, the magnitude of the risk would consist of the value of the cargo (which would be substantial), and more importantly, the value to the terrorists of successfully perpetrating another disastrous event with attendant media exposure and catastrophic setback for the global economy. The threat component in this risk-based analysis would consist of the terrorist capability in boarding a liquefied natural gas vessel whose vulnerability would be determined by a variety of factors. If the vessel is berthed pierside at a facility with a secure landside perimeter using proper fencing, qualified armed guards, closed-circuit television, and an alarm system that detects intruders, and the seaward side of the vessel is protected by armed small boat patrols and there is adequate lighting all around the vessel, the vulnerability to attack may be decreased enough to make the risk level acceptable.

The risk assessment for a weapons of mass destruction attack using an intermodal container would call for vulnerability mitigation that includes: effective container location and integrity sensing systems using radio frequency and satellite tracking equipment, an accurate database with shipper profile information, a container scanning and picture imprint capability at the cargo loading point of origin and at any transshipment point along the transportation route, and a Customs Service targeting analysis system capable of reacting quickly enough to prevent the loading of suspicious or high-risk containers.

Vulnerability mitigation for cruise vessels includes thorough baggage check procedures, effective credentialing and identification of passengers and crew, and an appropriate amount of physical security measures and armed security personnel and assets.

Another way to diminish the risk from terrorism in general is to erode the threat component by disrupting terrorist organizations and eliminating them wherever possible. The Bush administration's military efforts in Afghanistan, Yemen, Iraq, Pakistan, and other terrorist-infested areas have been an attempt to directly reduce the terrorist threat component. The process of eliminating the social, economic, and political roots of terrorism is critical to any attempt to contain its growth and development. If done effectively, the related results are long-lasting, if not permanent.

With respect to specific threats, terrorists may not have adequate knowledge of how to hijack a liquefied natural gas vessel and would prefer to crash airplanes into large buildings, because they have a history of success for these attacks. The mitigation of aviation vulnerabilities through the tightening of airport security and screening relative to those of maritime facilities and vessels works to increase the assessed risk of the latter. It discourages aviation attacks and causes the maritime scenarios to be more attractive to terrorists. Credible intelligence for terrorist threats may indicate an increase in risk based on the certainty of an attack. When the threat level is increased through intelligence reports, greater vulnerability mitigation is required to lower risk to an acceptable level. Multiple level or tiered security systems using military assets may be required to mitigate the vulnerability in a situation, so that acceptable levels of risk are achieved.

THE FUTURE OF MARITIME SECURITY

Much has been done to improve the level of maritime security in the United States since the events of September 11, 2001, but much more needs to happen before a satisfactory level of safety is reached. Requirements have been defined, responsibilities have been assigned, and funding has been made available, so that the security assessment process and the basic physical security infrastructure can be put into place. Sound intelligence analysis must indicate where additional programs and funding are required. The necessary effort must then be expended to ensure programs are implemented.

Many U.S. maritime security programs and initiatives are unsupported and untested. The U.S. maritime security program itself can be defined by critics as mitigation by legislation—which means laws have put policies in place with little or no funding to carry them out. Many organizational relationships must be forged, and new leadership personnel placed in several key positions in the emerging program, all of which are crucial to the safety of our country.

Additionally, some critics consider the threat from domestic supremacist sects and antiestablishment survivalist groups greater than that from Al Qaeda and its related terror organizations. In truth, both are serious threats and only time will reveal the magnitude of each. Notwithstanding these criticisms, now is the time we must proceed toward the creation of the long overdue U.S. maritime security program. The momentum and spirit toward this end, provided by the tragic events of September 11, 2001, must be vigorously sustained in order to prevent similar events from being repeated in the maritime industry.

LONG-TERM SECURITY SUPPORT

Given the existing vulnerabilities that have been revealed in the worst-case maritime scenarios and the associated funding required for their mitigation, a rigorous and rational cost-benefit analysis must be performed. Based on that analysis, the findings should be applied by government and industry to effect the capitalization of the most critical of these threats and vulnerabilities, so that scarce funding can be used more effectively across the intermodal transportation spectrum. Security capitalization would be based on the current terrorist threat, as deduced by accurate and appropriately coordinated national security intelligence.

The U.S. maritime security program, which has long suffered from a lack of funding and adequate support, now finds itself poised for progress. This progress will come complete with an effective plan, motivated leadership, an abundance of maritime awareness, vigilance, and training opportunities with which to maintain itself. The goal of effective security is almost within reach, as long as the recently awakened giant does not doze off again.

1789   U.S. Customs Service is established as part of the Treasury Department.

1790   U.S. Coast Guard established as a federal agency under the auspices of the Treasury Department.

1891   The U.S. Immigration and Naturalization Service is established.

1903   Immigration and Naturalization Service is transferred to the Department of Commerce and Labor.

1940   Immigration and Naturalization Service is transferred to the Department of Justice.

1941

December 7   Japan bombs U.S. Fleet at Pearl Harbor, Hawaii.

1961

January   *Santa Maria* is hijacked by Iberian Revolutionary Leadership Liberation Group terrorists on the way to Port Everglades, Florida, from Venezuela; shipping authorities capture and arrest the terrorists in St. Lucia.

1967   U.S. Coast Guard is transferred to the Department of Transportation.

1985

October   The *Achille Lauro* cruise ship is hijacked by Palestine Liberation Organization (PLO) terrorists on its way to Israel; the terrorists kill one passenger (Leon Klinghoffer) before surrendering to Egyptian authorities.

1987   During the Iran-Contra Scandal, Lieutenant Colonel Oliver North describes the operations of Osama bin Laden and his terrorist Al Qaeda network.

1991

December   The International Maritime Bureau's Office of Piracy Prevention is established in Kuala Lumpur, Malaysia.

1993

February 26   Terrorists bomb the World Trade Center in New York City, causing a large amount of damage and several casualties.

1995   Filipino police expose and prevent a terrorist plot (known as the Bojinka Plot) to blow up airplanes bound for the United States.

1998	The Federal Bureau of Investigation (FBI) receives information that indicates Osama bin Laden's terrorist organization may be planning to hijack airplanes and had found flaws in security at New York airports.
August	Clinton administration launches missile strikes against terrorist training facilities.
1999	
April 27	Clinton administration establishes the Clinton Port Security Commission to analyze threats to maritime and port security.
2000	
Spring	Senator Warren Rudman and Senator Gary Hart recommend the establishment of a Homeland Security Department.
August	Serbian commandos board the commercial ship *Delaware Bay* off the coast of Montenegro; through bribery, the captain convinces the terrorists to release the ship.
October	The U.S.S. *Cole* is heavily damaged in a terrorist suicide bombing while it refuels in the port of Aden, Yemen.
2001	
January	Florida passes strict codes for the regulation of maritime and port security.
April	Senator Fritz Hollings and Senator Bob Graham introduce Senate Bill S1412, which includes maritime safety recommendations based on the findings of the Clinton Port Security Commission.
May	President George W. Bush instructs Vice President Dick Cheney to take charge of establishing a counterterrorism system.
September 11	Al Qaeda terrorists crash commercial airplanes into the World Trade Center and Pentagon, causing massive casualties.
October	Congress passes the Transportation Security Act.
November	Coast Guard makes security recommendations in the immediate aftermath of 9/11.
2002	
January	The International Standards Organization (IMO) receives written recommendations, called "Prevention and Suppression of Acts of Terrorism against Shipping," from a U.S. Coast Guard commission.

February	Congress creates the Port Security Grants program.
April	The U.S. Customs Service's "Custom-Trade Partnership against Terrorism" (C-TPAT) is launched.
June	$93 million is awarded to qualified ports for port security assessments and related equipment; Bush administration unexpectedly announces its support for the creation of a new Homeland Security Department.
July	The Trade Act, requiring cargo manifest data to be transmitted to the Customs Service twenty-four hours before the cargo is shipped, is signed into law; Bush administration adds a proposal to the homeland-security strategy to be put into effect with the creation of the new Homeland Security Department; it suggests expanded extradition, the creation of terrorism insurance, and revised secrecy laws, among other things.
September 9	*Palermo Senator*, a Liberian container ship, is stopped off the coast of New Jersey and searched because readings indicating radioactive content onboard lead authorities to believe the ship might be carrying weapons of mass destruction; the radioactivity turns out to be caused by a container full of clay tiles; the ship is allowed to proceed.
October	The Patriot Act, which gives law enforcement authorities greater powers in tracking and interrogating suspects, is signed into law.
November	President George W. Bush signs the Maritime Transportation Security Act (formerly S1214) into law; Congress passes the Homeland Security Act, which provides for the formation of the new Homeland Security Department (which began in the fall of 2001 as the smaller Office of Homeland Security).
December	The International Standards Organization holds its annual meeting in London, England; at this conference, the IMO passes recommendations for the International Shipping and Port Security Codes that include the suggestions the U.S. Coast Guard had made the previous year; second round of Port Security Grants announced; terrorists blow up a French supertanker, the *Limberg*, as it enters port in Yemen.
2003	Transportation Secretary Norman Mineta announces a second phase of the Port Security Grants program that will provide seaports with additional funding to enhance security operations.

June 24   House of Representatives passes a homeland-security appropriations bill.

July 1   In the Federal Register, the U.S. Coast Guard publishes a list of possible maritime scenarios and their related levels of risk.

July 24   Joint Committee on Intelligence releases a report condemning the American intelligence community for errors that, had they been avoided, might have prevented the events of 9/11 from taking place.

Alderton, Patrick M., *Port Management Operations*. LLP Reference Publishing, 1999.

Branch, Alan E., *Elements of Shipping*. Stanley Thornes Ltd., 1996.

Fitzhugh, Thomas C. III, *International Perspectives on Maritime Security*. Department of Transportation, 1996.

Gray, Jim, Mark Monday, and Gary Stubblefield, *Maritime Terror: Protecting Your Vessel and Your Crew Against Piracy*. Paladin Press, 1999.

Hawkes, Gale, and Anthony Infante, *Port Security*. US Department of Transportation, 1998.

Hawkes, Kenneth Gale, *Maritime Security*. Cornell Maritime Press, 1989.

Joint Chiefs of Staff, *Handbook to Combating Terrorism*. Government Printing Office, 1996.

Kendall, Lane C., and James J. Buckley, *The Business of Shipping*. Cornell Maritime Press, 1994.

Maniscalco, Paul M., and Hank T. Chrislen, *Understanding Terrorism and Managing the Consequences*. Prentice Hall, Pearson Education, Inc., 2002.

Mizell, Louis R., Jr., *Target USA*. John Wiley and Sons, Inc., 1998.

Muller, Gerdhardt, *Intermodal Freight Transportation*. Eno Transportation Foundation, Inc., 1999.

Paratt, Brigadier (Ret.) Brian A.H., CBE, ed., *Violence at Sea*. ICC Publishing S.A., 1986.

Tyska, Lou, ed., *Guidelines for Cargo Security and Loss Control*. National Cargo Security Council, 2002.

BOOKS

Branch, Alan E., *Elements of Shipping.* Stanley Thornes Ltd., 1996.

Gardiner, Robert, and Alastair Couper, eds., *The Shipping Revolution: The Modern Merchant Ship.* Book Sales, 2000.

Gibson, Andrew, and Arthur Donovan, *The Abandoned Ocean: A History of United States Maritime Policy.* University of South Carolina Press, 2001.

Gray, Jim, Mark Monday, and Gary Stubblefield, *Maritime Terror: Protecting Your Vessel and Your Crew Against Piracy.* Paladin Press, 1999.

Hawkes, Kenneth Gale, *Maritime Security.* Cornell Maritime Press, 1989.

Kendall, Lane C., and James J. Buckley, *The Business of Shipping.* Cornell Maritime Press, 1994.

Maniscalco, Paul M., and Hank T. Chrislen, *Understanding Terrorism and Managing the Consequences.* Prentice Hall, Pearson Education, Inc., 2002.

Mizell, Louis R., Jr., *Target USA.* John Wiley and Sons, Inc., 1998.

WEB SITES

International Maritime Organization (IMO)
http://www.imo.org/home.asp
Works to encourage all maritime nations to adopt the best available standards to ensure maritime safety and efficiency.

International Maritime Security (IMS)
http://www.intmarsec.co.uk/
Private agency that provides security advice to the maritime industry.

Maritime Administration, Department of Transportation
http://www.marad.dot.gov/
Works to improve and strengthen the U.S. maritime system, including labor and infrastructure to meet the nation's economic and security needs.

The Maritime Security Council
http://www.maritimesecurity.org/
Works with federal and local government agencies to promote commercial vessel security.

United States Coast Guard—Maritime Security
http://www.uscg.mil/hq/g-m/nmc/security/
Includes links to published guidelines and regulations for maritime and port security.

ADDITIONAL RESOURCES

Unclassified maritime intelligence concerning threat information is available through several sources, including the Office of Naval Intelligence and the National Imagery and Mapping Agency. These two Department of Defense agencies provide accurate and up-to-date information regarding threats and criminal action against merchant shipping worldwide, which is available to the general public.

The Office of Naval Intelligence Civil Maritime Analysis Department produces a Worldwide Threat to Shipping Message that can be obtained by request at (301) 669-3261 or *cdragonette@nmic.navy.mil*. The report is carefully edited by Charles Dragonette, who, as a senior analyst and maritime security expert, has for many years provided industry and government officials with insight and analysis critical to the success of effective U.S. maritime security policy and procedure. In Dragonette's words, "Awareness of current maritime security events, where they are occurring and what measures are proving effective at control and prevention is a major step toward the kind of situational awareness that can spell the difference between success and failure in the safety of your ships, ports, personnel and cargo."

The National Imagery and Mapping Agency at *http://www.nima.mil* delivers antishipping activity information on their maritime safety information Web page and, in NIMA publication 117, also provides important emergency communications information.

Northern Command has been assigned the homeland-security mission within the Department of Defense and will be working with the U.S. Coast Guard to provide adequate defense against terrorist threats.

page:

i: Department of Defense photo by,
Photographer's Mate Second Class
Gloria J. Barry, Fleet Combat Camera
Group Pacific

ii: Department of Defense

iii: Courtesy of the U.S. Coast Guard

iv: U.S. Customs & Border Protection,
photo by James R. Tourtellotte

v: Courtesy of the U.S. General Accounting Office, 2003 Coast Guard Report

vi: Courtesy of the Maritime
Administration (MARAD)

vii: Courtesy of the U.S. General Accounting Office, 2002 Combating Terrorism
Report

viii: Courtesy of the U.S. Coast Guard

Captain Fred Evans is a Senior Associate at the U.S. Merchant Marine Academy Global Maritime and Transportation School where in 1992 he directed the development and implementation of the Maritime Security Course module in the U.S. Maritime Administration-sponsored National Sealift Training Program. He has since trained hundreds of mariners in shipboard and port and terminal security procedures. Prior to joining the staff at the USMMA GMATS and while on active duty with the U.S. Navy, Captain Evans performed service with the Chief of Naval Operations and Military Sealift Command Headquarters during Operation Desert Storm. Captain Evans also served as an in-theater Senior Naval Liaison Officer on the staff of Commander Joint Task Force Middle East and participated in twenty close escort missions aboard the Kuwaiti re-flagged U.S. tanker vessels during Operation Earnest Will and Operation Praying Mantis. Since the events of September 11, 2001, Captain Evans has directed, at the USMMA GMATS, the development and implementation of the Marine Terminal and Seaport Security Course and the Shipboard Security and Force Protection Course, which incorporate the proposed International Maritime Organization model courses for Facility Security Officer, Company Security Officer, and Ship Security Officer.

Larry C. Johnson is a recognized expert in the fields of counterterrorism, aviation security, and crisis and risk management. He has worked with the CIA and served as Deputy Director of the U.S. State Department's Office of Counterterrorism. In addition to his many published articles and interviews on television and radio, he has designed counterterrorism "war games" and represented the U.S. government at the OSCE Terrorism Conference in Vienna in 1996. He has played a key role in counterterrorism operations in the Middle East. Mr. Johnson currently is the chief executive officer of BERG Associates, LLC, an international consulting firm that helps multinational corporations and financial institutions manage the risks and counter the threats posed by terrorism and money laundering.